Provision

HOW GOD PROTECTS AND PROVIDES IN WAYS YOU COULD NEVER THINK OF

ROBERT PEMBERTON

authorHOUSE

AuthorHouse™
1663 Liberty Drive
Bloomington, IN 47403
www.authorhouse.com
Phone: 1 (800) 839-8640

Published by AuthorHouse 07/09/2020

ISBN: 978-1-7283-6658-6 (sc)
ISBN: 978-1-7283-6657-9 (e)

Library of Congress Control Number: 2020912552

Print information available on the last page.

This book is printed on acid-free paper.

This book is dedicated to

My family and friends. Rebecca, Phillip, James, Brice, Kayla and the grandkids, Jaden, Leila, Vincent and Eva. To those from my church family who stood with me through it all and are still there for me today. Pastor, Gladys, Jay, Selena, Claire, James, Linda, Karen, the women's prayer group, Steve, Ajanea, Carol, Derek, Ethan, Rudy, Micah, Teresa, Tom, Sharae, Maria, Brenda, Sylvia, LaRetta, Catherine, Lidia, Tara, Rob, Pete and Nancy.

To my new wife Terry who was sent from God to comfort me and give me new life. She has been amazing and vital to my strengthening. I know it was not easy for her to start a new relationship with me carrying so many good and bad memories into the marriage, but she has been wonderful and has helped me work through so many things I thought I had already handled.

God, family and my church are prevalent in my life. In the world we face daily, it is important to prioritize and to prioritize in the correct order. Provision comes to those who believe that God can provide, are open to His leading and willing to move when He says move. Unless your priorities are correct, I truly believe, you can miss what God has for you just because your focus is not on Him.

CONTENTS

Introduction..ix

Chapter 1 Setting the Stage.. 1
Chapter 2 All Good Things Must Come To An End.......................... 4
Chapter 3 The Medical Mystery Begins 6
Chapter 4 Now It Gets Serious...................................... 10
Chapter 5 The Day Everything Changed............................. 14
Chapter 6 Recovery Is Not Just Physical............................ 21
Chapter 7 Disease From Hell...................................... 25
Chapter 8 Beating The Monster Is A Fight........................... 29
Chapter 9 Trouble In The Midst Of Trouble 33
Chapter 10 Only God.. 37
Chapter 11 When God Doubled Down................................. 44
Chapter 12 Better or Worse?....................................... 50
Chapter 13 Time To Start Anew.................................... 55
Chapter 14 Provision To The End................................... 65
Chapter 15 Provision Of A Different Kind............................ 71
Chapter 16 Provision Is Blessing.................................... 78

About the Author.. 89

CONTENTS

Introduction ... ix

Chapter 1 Setting the Stage ...
Chapter 2 Alcohol: Thin Ribbon and How To Avoid It
Chapter 3 Metabolic Disorders Begin
Chapter 4 ... It Gets Worse ...
Chapter 5 The Day Everything Changed
Chapter 6 Recovery Is Not the Phase of
Chapter 7 Disease From Fat ...
Chapter 8 Beating Your Monster Is a Fight
Chapter 9 Troubled: The Wild Off Tracks
Chapter 10 Only Once ..
Chapter 11 Why Going Could Down
Chapter 12 Better or Worse ..
Chapter 13 This To Stay Away ..
Chapter 14 The Stop To the End ..
Chapter 15 Provision Of A Different Kind
Chapter 16 Promise in Bless and

About the Author ...

INTRODUCTION

No one ever expects devastation, it just happens. As you stand and watch life as you knew it disappear, the first reaction is to question what you have done wrong. When it comes to your faith, you start soul searching to identify what decisions you made or failed to make that got you out of alignment with God. There are quite a few mental battles that go along with the physical and /or financial battles you are facing. Without faith you can quickly become overwhelmed and hopeless. Even with faith the battles seem long and they seem to mount. Just when you thought it could not get any worse, wham, something new hits.

Having and maintaining faith through adversity is a challenge. I shudder to think how individuals who do not know the Lord and Father God must feel when facing life altering situations. Even with faith, keeping your eyes on Him and wholly trusting that He will make it all work out for your good is a challenge.

I decided to write this and share my journey. Not to get pity, not to elicit anger towards the worldly systems that failed us, but to demonstrate that no matter how bad or hopeless we think things are, God always has a way to see you through. He has ways you cannot conceive of.

As I go back and start at the beginning, back to 2013, I hope to show not only the challenges we faced but also how those challenges were answered with action and faith. Faith without action is dead. I also hope you will see that the Lord often does things that may not make sense at the time, but later you see how it was done to prepare you for what you are facing now.

CHAPTER ONE

Setting the Stage

T he marriage had gotten stormy. We did not see it coming. Over the years we had changed our expectations of each other and somehow never thought it was important enough to talk about it. Learning the hard way that communication is vital to any healthy relationship is painful. But we were there.

Married 31 years and in a trial separation, Lisa had bought a one-way ticket to go stay with her mother for a month. The kids had both graduated college and were starting their own lives in different cities and states. We were once again alone together but this time the together part was not the same.

I had grown so frustrated that I was ready for it to end. I convinced myself that I could accept whatever her decision was and I was not going to weigh in on the final decision. Mentally I was preparing myself for divorce proceedings which I knew meant I would lose everything. At that point I did not care anymore and my biggest mistake was I did not seek God. So wrapped up in believing it was over and pleading, not praying, that one of us would just go home to be with the Lord to end the turmoil and emotional pain, what the Lord wanted never came into consideration. I never once asked God, what should I do.

The phone rang and caller ID said it was Lisa. I answered preparing myself for the words that would change my life forever. But they did not come. Instead, I heard this,

"I have been praying about us and I don't want it to be over. The Lord does not want it to be over. I don't know how we got to here but I want us to be us again. I want to come back home and do whatever it takes to get through this. I love you and I am so sorry we are fighting. I don't want to fight. Can I buy a plane ticket and come back home?"

I was speechless. I had so mentally prepared myself for the Lord to

take her away either to Heaven or by divorce that I had never thought about what it would take to mend things. You see when faced with a problem, it is always easier to walk away than to take the time and effort solve it. So, if I was not a quitter in any other area of my life, why was I so willing to just quit at marriage? And if I truly believed that nothing is too hard for the Lord, why had I not asked Him what He wanted me to do rather than pleading for a solution my mind had contrived?

I told Lisa to buy the ticket. I told her we had to get to the bottom of this because I was unwilling to go on as we were when she left. She agreed and we talked about things we would have to talk about in detail when she returned. I began to ask the Lord, "so, what's next".

Several days later I went to the airport to pick her up. Unsure how to act, I gave her a hug and a quick kiss then got right to the task of retrieving luggage and heading us to the car. The ride home was filled with talk about family members, places visited and who was doing what back east. Nothing of substance was said. It was late in the day so upon arriving home I helped her unpack and we turned in for the night.

It was the weekend so when we awoke Saturday we started talking – talking about the hard stuff. In her prayer time the Lord had shown Lisa some areas where she had strayed and caused issues. We talked through them. In the process the Lord began to show me things I had done or not done that made the problem worse. We talked for hours, cleaning the slate of long buried unspoken hurts and revealing everything about our pasts, even before we had met. We agreed that anything and everything would be on the table and we loaded that table. When we were done, we prayed together. We had never done that. In 31 years of marriage we had never prayed together and certainly never prayed for one another and for our marriage, as a couple. This was the beginning of things to come.

In the weeks following, the healing that could only come from the Lord was evident every day. We grew closer, were more affectionate and basically fell in love all over again – this time with Christ as the center of the relationship. There was no verbal sparring, no innuendos and no snide remarks. Looks of disgust and bewilderment were replaced with smiles, I love yous and affection. Even the bedroom life turned up several notches

and this marriage was hitting on all cylinders and was supercharged. What was once a dread had turned into a dream and our marriage was Heaven on earth. We were closer to one another than ever and closer to the Lord as well. We would need that going forward.

All Good Things Must Come To An End

Both of us had gotten new jobs. I had been laid off from my company of 22 years and had spent a year trying to make it in selling and setting up church audio with an out of state company whose owner was a friend. In the 2013 economy, that was not going to work so I took a pay cut to break into the Oil and Gas industry which is prevalent in the Houston Texas area. Lisa's job as a nursing office assistant in the local school district had been eliminated so she moved to being an assistant in a Middle School counselling office handling records transfers between kids coming in from elementary school and those graduating to high school. Both of us were thrilled with our new jobs so the work side of things began to align with the personal side of things. Life was good. God was good. It was a fun time to be alive.

Like I said in the intro, no one ever expects devastation, it just happens.

Buyout rumors and layoff rumors went from being rumors to being evident in my job. I decided I would work my way through them. Try to become indispensable, you know. Maybe if I just did well enough they would pick someone else when the time came. Her job began to sour some as well when districtwide job shuffles combined with school level personnel changes made for an ever changing and uncomfortable situation.

Lisa began to complain of extreme fatigue and occasional forgetfulness. Her back seemed to hurt all the time and we were at our chiropractor almost weekly. We both thought it was stress caused by the unrest on both of our jobs. Nonetheless, we began the medical route to have a complete physical and see if there was a physical cause for the changes. Everything on paper seemed good so we were back to blaming everything on stress.

Then I got the call at work. It was Lisa's office and they were asking

what emergency room did I want to meet them at. While sitting at her desk she had become confused, could not answer simple questions and just seemed to not be there. The staff knew something was wrong but did not know where to take her. I gave them the name of a local hospital close to our home and agreed to meet them there. Someone from the staff was going to drive her and I would arrange to get her car later. Since my manager was in Germany, I sent an email explaining there was a medical emergency and I left work for the hospital.

When I arrived, Lisa was confused and complaining that nothing felt right. They immediately began testing and soon found that the thyroid substitute that a local doctor had convinced her to try was not working at all and since she had an irradiated thyroid, she was essentially getting no thyroid function. The treatment plan was to start synthetic thyroid and send her to an endocrinologist. This is where the God connections began.

The Medical Mystery Begins

The next day, at work, I was talking to a friend and explaining why I had to leave so suddenly. My friend was not familiar with thyroid issues so I began to explain to her what was going on. An older engineer (he was retirement age but was working because he enjoyed what he did) sitting across the room came over to my desk and he said, I really was not ease dropping on your conversation but I heard the magic word – thyroid. He said my wife works in thyroid cancer research and she knows just about everyone in the area who is anyone in endocrinology. Do you have a doctor?

I told him we did not and he asked if I would mind talking with his wife. I agreed and the next day she called and we talked medical for the better part of an hour. She concluded that my wife needed to see a specialist because the symptoms were not completely consistent with wrong thyroid levels in the blood. She suspected from our conversation that something else was at play so she asked which area of town we lived in. Based upon that she recommended a young endocrinologist who she said was one of the brightest she had worked with. We were able to get an appointment in weeks, not months. That in itself is a miracle these days.

The initial visit was routine and both of us immediately took to and trusted the new doctor. Though the doctor agreed that something seemed off, the course of action was to get the thyroid under control, establish a stable dose of medication and monitor the "other symptoms" as we went. For the next several months we would go for bloodwork and return visits until thyroid indicators stabilized in Lisa's system. The "other symptoms" continued to worsen. There was pain in the back and under her ribs and strange sensations in her extremities. Sense of touch seemed to be dulling and fatigue continued to get worse even with wholesale diet changes and regular exercise and sleep routines.

We decided that maybe some light exercise would help with the fatigue feeling so we decided to do evening walks through our neighborhood. There is a sidewalk path at the end of our street that makes a 3.5 mile loop so we started walking the loop. After a few days of this, Lisa would get about a half mile in then tell me she needed to stop. I encouraged her to push through thinking this was like the wall that distance runners face. Every half mile she would stop then after a few minutes of rest she would go again. I was getting frustrated thinking she was just being lazy but she kept insisting that there was something that was physically preventing her from going more than a half mile at a time. The strange part was that after the stop for a minute of two, she felt fine until the next episode hit forcing her to rest again.

When we visited endocrinology, we asked if this was part of thyroid issues. Our doctor quickly (as in a few months) determined there was something else going on and she suggested a visit to neurology. She knew of a neurologist locally that she had attended med school with and she described her as "scary smart". So, she made the call and once again we got an appointment in weeks not months. The "brightest I've ever worked with" had now referred us to "scary smart". You could say we were seeing the best.

It only took one visit to neurology and several series of tests to determine that something was indeed not right but it was not obvious what. The pain in the back and under the ribs was now so prevalent that Lisa was living on Advil to get through the day. Our chiropractor told her that she was wasting her money coming back to him because the source of the pain was not caused by spinal misalignment. He suggested Lisa see neurology which we told him we were already doing. So, on the second visit to neurology, after all the test results were in, we were told once again that something was not normal but it was not obvious what it was. The recommendation was to see a neuromuscular disease specialist at University of Texas Medical Center. Our neurologist ("scary smart") had studied with another doctor who she described as "the smartest person I have ever met". Once again, she made the call and we had a consult within a week.

All this time both of us are continuing to work and trying our best to schedule appointments in the afternoon so we could go in early and

work as much time as possible to avoid using vacation time or losing pay. My work was intense as I was root causing technical issues that were costing my company millions of dollars in tool downtime. I was working daily with calls and video conferences between Houston and Germany while working in interview/observation visits to local sites. Management wanted me to be the lead on a team that would redefine the tool development process from end to end tying in lessons learned and financials from previous projects. When done, we were to write a technical paper and submit it for international publication review. So, by day I was Black Belt Engineer and by night a medical researcher studying up on everything doctors said they were considering. Lisa continued to work her office job taking Advil for pain and trying to exercise or do anything that might relieve the pain.

The consult with neuromuscular disease was pleasant and we both felt a connection to the new doctor. She was smart, thorough, fashionable, personable and concerned. She ordered a series of tests on top of the thorough exam and when we went back the next week she had concluded that we were looking at mild case of myasthenia gravis. This could explain the strange neurological anomalies but not the pain in the back and ribs. We started medication and agreed to monitor the other symptoms. We were to come back in a month for another visit.

The next week the pain grew so intense that we went to the ER. While conducting blood work, the ER doctors discovered that Lisa's gall bladder was not functioning. They called in a surgeon who recommended immediate surgery to remove it and we agreed. The surgery went well but only some of the pain was relieved. Now Lisa had stomach pain in addition to rib and back pain. They thought the pain under the ribs was caused by the bad gall bladder so everyone was shocked that it had not subsided much after the surgery. Back at the hospital for a post-surgical visit, the surgeon wanted to do an upper GI scope. We agreed and he found multiple ulcers. He said that living on Advil to cut pain had literally eaten a hole in Lisa's stomach. The Advil was stopped immediately and replaced with several stomach and digestive meds. She was released to home.

Through all of this, we never missed church. As audio director and bass player in the praise team, I was there for every service and practices

too. Lisa would come to practices and attend group prayer services in another part of the building. She volunteered for the greeting ministry team and the alter cloth ministry. So, our week consisted of church several times, medical appointments and our jobs. We had to make time for each other on our one day off, Saturday. Still, we were in this together and we knew that God had a plan thought it was hard to see what. In the midst of the battle we often are so focused on the battle that we cannot conceive there is a bigger plan. We knew all of this was an attack from the enemy. We suspected that the enemy had wanted our marriage dissolved and because we had come together in the Lord and made it stronger than ever, we accepted this battle knowing with the Lord we would win.

CHAPTER FOUR

Now It Gets Serious

It was a Thursday night and I had gone to praise team practice. Lisa stayed home because she had gotten home late from work and needed to rest. When I walked through the door coming home after practice, Lisa was sitting in the living room floor. Being just two weeks post-surgery from gall bladder removal I thought this was strange. When I asked what she was doing she said she was on the way to the laundry room and her legs stopped working. She was unable to get up. I grabbed her under each armpit and proceeded to lift her up. When I did she screamed in pain and said her back was really hurting. I got her ready for bed and told her to rest. We were to go for a post-operative visit in the morning and figured we could ask the doctor what he thought.

The next day, Lisa could hardly move her legs and she said they felt numb and heavy. Me being a survivor of Guillain Barre Syndrome, I immediately suspected GBS or something neurological. I helped her get dressed and we went to the post-op visit. On the way into the office I had to all but carry her. While she was visiting the surgeon, I called our neuromuscular specialist and asked if this was some advanced symptom of myasthenia gravis. The doctor said no and suggested I drive her downtown for an exam immediately after the visit where we were. This was the Friday before Labor Day and most offices were closing early.

Leaving the office of the post-op visit I had to assist Lisa to the car like you would support someone with a leg injury. I drove downtown to the Houston Medical Center and decided to valet park so we would be closer to the elevators than if we had parked in the garage. The way she was having trouble walking I was wondering if I should request a wheelchair to get her to the office. As we entered the lobby, someone from security saw us and brought us a wheelchair without asking and we were grateful. Once I got her into the wheelchair we went up to the doctor office.

Upon arrival, we were taken directly to an exam room and several staff members joined the doctor while I was asked to wait. We found out later that most of the staff had left to start the holiday weekend and the doctor had called them and asked that they come back and assist her. Now how often does that happen these days? Provision.

The doctor came out to talk to me and she was a little more serious than I had ever seen her. She said, "To answer your question you asked me on the phone, no, this is not a severe symptom of myasthenia gravis. This is neurological and she is not going home. I will have someone bring you another wheelchair and I want you to walk her across the connector bridge over Fannin and go to admitting at Memorial Hermann. I have made the call and someone will meet you there".

"What's wrong?", I asked.

"I cannot say for sure but I suspect it is neurological so they will probably admit her and run more tests. We need a MRI for certain and I'll let the admitting doctors decide where to go from there. As soon as the wheelchair gets here, you need to take her right over."

"Is it that serious?", I asked.

"It's out of my hands now", she said, "I trust the doctors who will meet you."

At this point my brain was on fire. On the outside trying to stay positive, cool and supportive but inside feeling like a squirrel in traffic. Neurologic did not sound good and the symptoms I was observing were not something you could just live with. I was anxious, scared and praying for answers.

So, the wheelchair arrived and we took off across the connector bridge, down the elevator and directly to admitting. After another short wait and signing the usual insurance and admitting paperwork, we were met by medical personnel who escorted us upstairs to her room. No sooner had we arrived at the room when a gurney arrived and they told me she was being taken for a MRI. I could sit in the room and wait for them to come back. It felt good to sit down for a moment but was also very unnerving to not know what was going on or even where we were.

I walked into the hallway and asked nurse as she passed by, "where are we?"

"Memorial Hermann Hospital", she replied.

"I know that much, but what floor is this? Is this a specialty floor or a med surge floor?"

"This is the neurology floor", she replied.

I thought to myself, well that makes sense since the doctor said she thought this was a neurology problem. I sat back down in the room and turned on the TV. My mind was racing so much that even the TV news seemed settling. It was not long at all before Lisa was wheeled back into the room and settled in bed. The nursing staff came in and did the usual vitals and medical history check in and got us settled.

No sooner had they finished when two doctors walked into the room. To my surprise the younger of the two took the lead and introduced himself as a trauma neurosurgeon.

"You've got to be kidding me," I thought under my breath. Trauma and neurosurgery? She just fell on the floor, she was not in a car wreck.

He said the MRI revealed a larger tumor on her thoracic spinal column that had grown through the vertebrae on both sides and was now pressing against the spinal cord. He was recommending immediate surgery where he would remove the outer portion of her vertebrae and then cut the tumor from the spinal cord and place rods to stabilize the spine. Surgery would be in the morning as he expected it to take nearly 12 hours and it was already Friday evening. He explained the dangers associated with such a surgery and said he needed permission to proceed before assembling and notifying the surgical team.

Stunned is not a strong enough word to describe how either of us felt. Neither of us drove down here to consider surgery much less one that could cause permanent damage. We talked it over and there really was no alternative – remain unable to use your legs while something continued to grow inside you or cut it out and risk not being able to walk. We had to opt for surgery.

We signed the consent forms then I got on the phone and called the kids. How do you tell your children that their mother in a hospital unable to walk with something growing through her spinal cord and will require neurosurgery in less than 12 hours? There is no easy way to break that news so you just make the call and state the facts. My daughter who is a BSN nurse and my son who is a computer engineer in defense/ aerospace both asked if they should come. I left it up to them but both

headed this way immediately. One from hours away and the other by plane from another state. By midnight, both were with me and we went to bed not knowing what tomorrow would bring. As I went to bed I do not remember what I prayed or if I prayed at all that night. Mind racing and wishing it was over faded into sleep until the alarm went off.

CHAPTER FIVE

The Day Everything Changed

I'm not sure if I really slept or if my brain rehearsed every possible outcome of what was about to happen while I was in some altered state. I felt like I had not slept combined with the adrenaline rush of starting a race. The start of that day is still a blur and I do not recall things like what/if we had breakfast or how many cars we drove to the hospital. We all showed up to Lisa's room as she was being prepped to go to the operating room. She was excited to see the kids and thanked them for coming as she began to cry. Who knows if they were tears of joy, love or fear or all of the above. We got there in time to escort her down to the operating room then after kisses and goodbyes we were sent to a waiting area that was set up for people who are going to be waiting a while. We were told that about 4 hours into surgery someone would come and brief us on progress. The doctor came out to meet us then he disappeared behind locked doors. We decided to walk around and explore the area to see where everything was like restrooms, cafeteria, gift shop, exits to outside, etc. No sooner had we returned when I saw her doctor coming out with another gentleman by his side. I thought, "This cannot be good".

The neurosurgeon explained that because of the holiday, his regular surgical team was not there so they had assembled another team. The anesthesiologist who was on call had attempted to insert a central line through the carotid artery and had accidentally exited the artery and punctured Lisa's lung with the line. Surgery would be canceled and she would be sent to ICU until the extent of the damage was determined. This was not a good start and I began to doubt our decision to move forward. None the less, we followed her back upstairs and this time to ICU where she was taken away for a different series of scans and tests. Eventually she was returned to her room where we were all anxious to see her.

The results of the tests showed no major damage but because of the

danger of the lung collapsing, Lisa would remain in ICU through the weekend and surgery would be rescheduled for early Tuesday morning anticipating no setbacks over the weekend.

Now this apparent setback turned out to actually be a blessing. You see, by delaying until Tuesday, the trauma neurosurgeon would be well rested and his support team would be his regular team he used during trauma operations. During the wait I was able to research the trauma neurosurgeon and find out he was one of only a very few in the country who were qualified and trained to perform a surgery where a tumor would be cut from the spinal cord. As I read about how the surgery would be done, the engineer in me was fascinated and the husband side of me prayed that God would guide his hands and make all go well. God had guided our every step to date and providing one of the best trauma neurosurgeons in the country and arranging for him to operate well rested and with full support staff was just another blessing.

Tuesday morning started just as Saturday morning had. We met Lisa at the room then escorted her down to the OR and took our place in the waiting area. We were assigned an OR nurse who would monitor the procedure and come to give us periodic updates. She was a woman about my age who was a traveling nurse. Her and Rebecca hit it off immediately and began to talk about nursing and career moves. The traveling nurse was to the point and pulled no punches when talking to Rebecca. She cut her no slack and really got her thinking. In the process of conversation, she met Phillip and was surprised that he was single. She talked about her daughter who was about his age who traveled with her. Before I knew it, Phillip had come out of his shell and asked if her daughter would want to talk to him. This was a total shock to all of us who had watched Phillip grow up and take no initiative to start a friendship. The nurse texted her daughter and asked if she was interested in talking to Phillip and when she said yes, the daughter and Phillip exchanged phone numbers and began texting. For the rest of the day, Phillip was preoccupied with his new text friend and Rebecca was preoccupied with researching different nursing options. God once again had intervened and provided something for the kids to focus on besides the operation.

About 6 hours in, the trauma neurosurgeon appeared. He had successfully removed the external tumor and the exterior bone at T7

and they were taking a break before doing the more delicate part of shaving the tumor off of the spinal cord. He said all was going well but there is always concern when someone is under anesthesia that long laying face down with the table tilted downward. If anything, taking a break and flattening out the table would allow the body to return to normal circulation for a while before beginning again. The medical science involved was fascinating but scary as well. I just wanted it to be over and successful.

The afternoon seemed to drag on forever and I became almost obsessed with watching the windows for signs of the traveling nurse or the trauma neurosurgeon. Rebecca and James were walking around talking and Phillip had agreed to meet his new text friend at the park across from the hospital. I wish I could tell you that I was in payer and talking to the Lord but I admit I was preoccupied with the present surroundings and getting agitated. About then the trauma neurosurgeon came out and talked to me, Rebecca and James. We texted Phillip and told him we would text him Lisa's next location as soon as we knew where we were going.

We were told the surgery had gone very well even though it took 11 ½ hours. They had gotten as much of the tumor as they could and the rest (any residual on the spinal cord and the part in the internal segment of the T7 vertebrae) would be treated with radiation. The tumor had been sent to the lab for testing to see what it was. The initial diagnosis was solitary plasma cytomas – a single tumor of unknown origin.

Because half of the T7 vertebra had been removed, support rods had been placed on either side of the spine. Normally they would attach 2 vertebrae above and below (T5 and T9), but the MRI showed unusual density in T5 so to be safe that the screws would not pull out, the rods were attached a T3 and T9 – effectively fusing her entire thoracic spine. Since Lisa had scoliosis, he did not want to suddenly force her spine to be straight so the rods were bent to match the curve of her spine while providing a minor amount of straightening. She would be in a wraparound "Turtle shell" brace that would be custom fit once swelling went down in a day or so. Until then she would remain in ICU under mild sedation. I shook the doctor's hand and thanked him and the traveling nurse led us to the recovery room where Lisa was coming out of anesthesia. We were

warned that she may not be able to talk to us but was waking up. What happened next was not at all what we expected.

Me, Rebecca and James went to her recovery area but only 2 at a time were allowed in so James agreed to stay outside for the first visit. When we saw her, she was on her back which surprised me and her face was swollen. She was staring into space with eyes freakishly wide open and she was calling out in what can only be described as an encounter with the Lord and a prophecy.

Lisa: Help me! Help me! Get me out of here! You have to get me out of here! I'm drowning!

Me: You're not in water. You're in a hospital bed.

Lisa: I'm floating! I'm floating away! Get me out of here! Help me! Help me!

Me: You are safe. You're in a hospital bed. You just had surgery and you're waking up. Nothing is going to happen to you. I'm right here.

Lisa: I'm floating! Don't let me die! I'm floating away!

Me: Lisa you are not even in water. You're in a hospital bed and me and Rebecca are here with you.

Lisa: Let me die! Please let me die! I don't want this! Let me go! Please let me go!

Rebecca leaves the room crying.

Me: You're not going to die. You're not floating. You're in a hospital bed and you just had back surgery.

Lisa: Please (long silent pause) oh, you are beautiful.......

Me: Who are you talking to?

Lisa: God! He's right here! He's right here. I see Him. He's here. Let me go with you. Please take me with you. I want to go with you. Please!

I look at the monitors and all vital signs are normal and stable.

Lisa: What do you mean I'm not done? What else do I have to do? I don't want to go. (Pause in the speaking) I'm healed by the stripes and blood of Jesus. Satan you're a liar! I'm floating. I'm floating! I have to get them off of that boat! They're going to be killed! We have to get them off of that boat!!!!

Rebecca comes back into the room.

Lisa: Those boats are going to crash and the babies are going to die!!!! My babies! I have to get my babies off of that boat!!!!

Me: Lisa our kids are grown. Rebecca and Phillip are out of college. What babies?

Lisa: Our grandkids. Our grandkids are on that boat! I have to save the babies!

Me: It's ok. They are safe. They are not on the boat. I'm sorry but how is it I did not know those babies were our grandkids? Who had them?

Lisa: Rebecca and James.

Me: How many?

Lisa: Four. She had twins and two more.

Me: How do you know this?

Lisa: God is showing me the future. (Pause) Where is Phillip?

Me: He is across the street in the park.

Lisa: I need to see him.

Me: I can call him but it may take a while to get up here. He went there to meet a girl he has been texting this afternoon. He went to meet your nurse's daughter.

Lisa: I see them. They have to get off of those boats. Those boats are going to crash and wrap around them! Those boats are going to wrap around them!! Those babies are going to die if you don't get them off of that boat!!

Me: We got the grandkids and they are safe. I said thinking if she could hear me this might snap her out of the fear

Lisa: There are more babies!

Me: Who had them?

Lisa: Phillip.

Me: How many?

Lisa: Three.

Me: With who?

Lisa: Maria.

Me: We don't know anyone named Maria.

Lisa: No. That's not right. Not Maria. I don't know her name. I have not met her.

Me: Philip will come see you soon. He is safe.

Lisa: They have to stay off of those boats. They're going to wrap around. Get that off of her neck! It's wrapping around her neck!!

Me: What is wrapping around her neck, the boat?

Lisa: No! It's a chord and it's wrapping around her neck. You have to get it off!

Me: Who is the chord wrapping?

Lisa: Phillip's wife.

Me: Ok I got it. They are safe. There is no chord and there are no boats. Everyone is safe I said, again hoping she would hear and snap out of this

Lisa: I need to die for what I have done.

Me: You did not do anything. Why do you think you deserve to die? What do you think you did?

Lisa: I killed my father.

Me: No, you didn't. He died of cancer. I was there in the room when he died. You could not have killed him, the cancer did.

The next part I am not telling because it is very personal and really does not need to be discussed outside of immediate family so I will fast forward in the recovery episode.

Lisa: I deserve to die for what I did.

Me: Someone is lying to you. You did not kill anyone. Tell whoever is talking that they are a liar and everyone knows it. You just said God told you that you are not done. You're not going to die until God says so. He is the only one who can say when you will die.

Lisa: I'm floating. Get me out of this water! That boat is going to hit them! The chords are going to wrap. They will get stuck on the anchors. The anchors are going to pull them down. They will get tangled.

Me: There is no water. You are not in water. There is no boat. You are in the hospital and the drugs are making you see things.

Lisa: The boat is leaning! It's going to tip over!

Me: What boat? Where are you?

Lisa: Fishing. We're fishing.

Me: Where is the boat you are fishing from?

Lisa: Galveston. We're fishing in Galveston.

Me: Did you catch anything?

Lisa: Yes, a lot.

Me: How many did you catch?

Lisa: 150,000. Mom had to take some because they were damaging the house. She had to take some and clean them.

Me: Well it sounds like there was enough that everyone can have some.

Lisa: We have to nail those fish to the boat.

Me: Why?

Lisa: The boat is tipping over and the fish will fall off if we don't nail them down.

Me: It seems like you caught enough so why do we have to nail them down?

Lisa: We have to keep them so we can give them away.

Me: Who are you fishing with?

Lisa: Rick.

Me: Who is Rick?

Lisa: James's dad. He's got shoes.

Me: What kind of shoes?

Lisa: Flip flops. He sells them. He has them in his shirt and he sells them.

At this point Rebecca and I are laughing but trying not to. This story had gone from meeting God and saving future babies to a fishing trip where James' dad was selling shoes out of his shirt. Lisa stopped talking and we told her to get some rest. Each of us gave her a kiss and walked outside he room just as Phillip was arriving back from his park meeting. He told us the meeting was fun but it was obvious they were not each other's type and now he wanted to know how his mom was doing. He went in to see her and to hold her hand for a while. She was now resting and we waited for her to be released back to neuro ICU. The day everything changed was coming to a close.

CHAPTER SIX

Recovery Is Not Just Physical

After such a major surgery, you have to walk that fine line between rest for recovery and movement to be able to return to normal. Amidst the excitement and confusion of the surgery, none of us thought to ask about the recovery process or even if she would regain use of her legs. So, there we were visiting in the room with no clue as to what was next until the trauma neurosurgeon came to the room on rounds and spoke to us after examining the incision and the surgical site. In a few days Lisa would be fitted for the "Turtle shell" and upon discharge she would be transferred to TIRR – The Institute for Rehabilitation Research to learn to walk again. This came as a shock because TIRR had an international reputation and also quite the waiting list. The fact that we could transfer from Memorial Hermann directly to TIRR was yet another blessing. The Lord was continuing to line up the best and clear the path to see who we needed and be where we needed to be. And above all of that, my job was allowing me to come in early and leave early to drive the 35 miles to the Medical Center after work each night.

Lisa was in ICU for a few days then transferred to neuro step down unit then discharged to TIRR which was literally around the corner from the hospital. By this time the kids had gone back to their respective cities and I would send a text update to them each evening stating progress for that day. Lisa and I settled into yet another new routine at yet another new facility.

During the day she would have multiple sessions of physical therapy. There was very little rest as she was worked hard to restrengthen muscles, teach the body to once again do walking motions and take classes on how to care for herself in a brace and/or wheelchair. By the time I would get there in the late afternoons, she was exhausted but happy to see me. Sometimes I would wheel her outside so she could get fresh air and

sunshine. Other days we would go to the mat room and she would show me what she had learned about how to get in/out of the chair and how to roll over in the shell or get in/out of the shell to clean up. Other times we would just rest and watch TV together until I had to drive home and do it all over again. Weekends were spent by her side in the room but PT did not stop on the weekends so I got to watch and learn. Sundays I would play in the praise band at church in the morning, drive down to visit after service then drive back to play the evening service. Lisa would watch Sunday mornings on livestream then ask me on Monday evening what the Sunday evening sermon was. Through it all, we did our best to stay connected to our church.

As the weeks went by, she was fitted for a custom wheelchair, walker and cane. We continued to believe there would be the obvious progression from wheelchair back to walking as she got stronger and the swelling around the spinal cord continued to go down.

I do not remember if we prayed together but I know every night I would pray for her full recovery and she would start every day with Bible reading and prayer. She found a book on healing scriptures and would read and declare them over herself every day. She always wanted me to tell Pastor and Sister Gladys how much she missed them and how glad she would be to get back to church. One time when I was giving them an update, they asked if she could have visitors. They wanted to surprise her. So, I contacted the staff at TIRR and had them added to the approved visitor list.

I was not there the day they visited because I was at work and they went before I could get off to get there. But I heard about the visit both from Lisa and from my pastors.

As you turn past the check-in desk at TIRR there is a long hallway that leads you past the classrooms and rehab rooms. Pastor and Gladys were walking this hallway when they spotted Lisa sitting in a classroom in her wheelchair. After a few moments they saw each other and Lisa broke out in tears of joy when they entered the classroom. They sat with her until class was over then wheeled her to a place where they could visit. The Holy Spirit showed up and Lisa began to minister to our pastors declaring the greatness of God, His mercy and His love. To their amazement she was ministering to them when they had come to minister to her. Being

confined to a wheelchair and having to prepare for life in a new way had drawn her closer to the Lord and made her more appreciative for each day no matter what the challenge.

The visit from our pastors was just the boost she needed to face what was next which we thought would end with multiple sessions of 3D conformal radiation to kill the rest of the tumor. After 3 weeks in TIRR we were finally coming home – in a wheelchair with limited use of a walker. Our new schedule would involve balancing my job with outpatient physical therapy sessions in Memorial City, 3D conformal radiation treatments and oncology visits at the Medical Center. She tried to help out around the house but I was nervous about her cooking and moving hot/boiling things. I had to learn to let go so she could learn to cope.

As soon as she was released, we were back in church. I got so good at expanding and collapsing the wheelchair that I could do it in my sleep so going to church, the store or appointments seemed routine with the wheelchair. All the while she was getting stronger and learning to walk again. Our church family celebrated each step with us as from week to week they could see her move from wheelchair, to walker to cane. The effects of the support of our church, the spiritual boost Lisa received from out pastors visiting and the daily reading of healing scripture were evident as she quickly progressed through radiation and outpatient PT and back to walking.

Once she was stable enough to walk all terrain with a cane, we began to take longer and longer walks through our neighborhood. This was great for strengthening and balance but she began to complain that walking on an uneven surface was really making her lower back ache. The surgery had been in the upper spine so why would the lower back hurt?

In the meantime, test results on the tumor had come back as well as blood tests for cancer. MRIs showed that the radiation had decimated the remaining tumor in the T7 vertebrae and the residual traces of a cancer marker in the blood were determined to be from the dying tumor. The tumor was deemed noncancerous. We were told all looked great and we should come back for a check-in in 6 months. During that 6 months the lower back pain continued to worsen and our evening walks got shorter

and shorter. We decided to go back to the trauma neurosurgeon and see if anything that was done to the C-spine could be causing pain in the lower back. He examined her and said there was nothing abnormal at the C-spine but suggested we go back and talk to oncology.

Once again, we were able to get a same week appointment with oncology and they wanted us to go for labs since were already in the Medical Center to see our surgeon. So off to the labs it was and then home to wait for the next appointment.

Disease From Hell

I n the midst of all that was happening personally, there was also trouble developing on the job front. My management chain was in another country and I could sense a shakeup was coming. They were using our Houston based resources to develop new processes then seeing that those new processes were immediately implemented in the factory in their home company before we could roll them out locally. I could sense, or it was a Holy Spirit witness, that they were going to improve operation in their home country then transfer the work to that site and leave us out to dry.

I began looking for a new position within the company to get ahead of what I knew would happen. Being proactive is good right? Except when the culture of your management chain demands total loyalty to your managers. Looking for new positions, and the next two levels of management had to be notified every time you applied for something new, was viewed as disloyalty and they began to block any attempts to move to a new position. I began to get calls from them asking why I was looking around and they moved up deadlines that we had previously agreed to. I did not need this added pressure with everything else going on.

I went to HR and explained the situation – both professional and personal. On the professional side there was little that could be done because I had been in my current position less than 2 years so any move had to be approved by current manager. They could block me from moving. On the personal side, I was instructed to file paperwork for FMLA to cover me in case I needed time off to care for Lisa beyond my allotted flexible time off. No sooner had I filed paper work when what I predicted happened. Our local work was moved to the home country of my manager and director. They both received promotions for the

improvements "they had made" and me and the rest of the local staff were assigned to whatever positions that looked like a match.

I immediately scheduled a meeting with my new manager to see what I would be doing and to alert him to Lisa's condition and my need for flexibility in getting her to appointments. He was very understanding and he allowed me to come in as early as 6 AM and work through lunch so I could leave in time to get Lisa to downtown Houston for late afternoon appointments. After a few weeks he went even further and said as long as my assignments were getting completed on time and he was kept up to date on progress, he really did not care what hours I put in. Little did I know at the time what a blessing that would become. God was providing in advance and I never saw it.

So, the day to meet back with oncology arrived and we were there on time in spite of my work day and the drive. Our oncologist was also a professor who taught doctors in the oncology field. Once again, the Lord had provided the best. He was usually very upbeat and made jokes with us. Not today. He walked in with an assistant and was very solemn. I knew at that point that what was coming could not be good.

"The lab tests came back and the results are not good. What we thought was residual cells from irradiating the tumor was actually cancer and it has gotten much worse over the past 6 months. You have multiple myeloma cancer and we have to start aggressive treatment immediately."

What the h____ is multiple what??? My brain went to fog and all I could hear was cancer got worse over six months. When I regained focus he was saying Lisa would need IV chemotherapy three times a week and blood draws would have to happen before each to see if she could stand the treatment. Treatment days would include weekends as necessary. He said they could should start treatments that day. That grace at work with flexibility in schedule was about to be put to the test.

Over the next few weeks I was like a grad student preparing to write a thesis. Almost every spare moment at work and at home in the evenings was spent studying up on Multiple Myeloma, treatments, cell biology, our oncologist's background, you name it. I had to understand what was just dropped on us and understand it well enough that I could talk intelligently with oncology and others about what they were proposing for treatments. I wanted to know what was expected and what was not

during treatment so I could advocate for Lisa when necessary. I just knew I had my part to play in this though I did not know what that part was. When you take a vow before God to be there for better or worse, in sickness and in health you better mean it. I was suddenly facing worse and sickness all at the same time.

Outpatient treatments began. After check-in and treatment chair assignment, blood was drawn and sent to the lab. That usually took about 2 hours to come back which was immediately frustrating to me. I thought, there has to be a more efficient way than this. I would soon learn that in cancer treatment, the treatment and results trumped efficiency every time. So, after waiting for labs which showed white cell counts and hemoglobin levels, we were approved for treatment which involved IV and injections. Afterward there was a waiting period to assure there was no adverse reaction. Occasionally, the labs would come back too low and treatment was rescheduled. A few times the labs came back so low that Lisa was given a blood transfusion followed by a treatment. The treatment process was repeated 3 times a week for about 3 months. At this point the exact time lines are starting to fade from memory.

After a few months of the weekly routine I asked our oncologist what the end game was. Were we just supposed to keep up these treatments indefinitely? The answer was no, the end goal was to beat the cancer down low enough that Lisa could transfer to MD Anderson and be prepared for a bone marrow transplant. More researching on my part. But in the meantime, the pain of having your bone marrow destroyed by cancer was starting to mount. We were sent to pain management specialists but something was wrong.

The initial medications were opioid pain killers which were hard to get and each new dose brought new symptoms and reactions to deal with. Without going into excruciating detail of which drug did what, let's just say this was not a pleasant journey. It went something like this. Pain is not controlled so you schedule an appointment with pain management and drive downtown. You talk to the doctor who changes the dose (usually increasing it) and hands you a new prescription. You then search for a pharmacy in the Medical Center or in vicinity to your home that is on your insurance and can fill heavy narcotics. You go home and get food so the meds do not rip apart your stomach then you take the new meds

and hope they work better than the previous ones. Sometimes it's a hit and you are ok for a while and at other times it is immediately obvious that this is not going to work so you start over with another appointment.

At one point we were calling after hours numbers at 2 AM because the pain was so bad and uncontrolled. On a few occasions I had to drive her to the ER to receive pain treatment. The final straw came when the third call at 2 AM in one week which resulted in the same instructions – increase the dose – resulted in opioid overdose. Lisa woke up and could not walk. Sitting on the couch while I called doctor offices and got recordings and promises to call back, she began to slide sideways and was trying to lay feet up and head down on the couch. I asked her what was going on and she said everything was upside down and floating. When I finally got a doctor on the phone he said the dose was too high and we would have to try yet another drug.

The next week we were accepted into MD Anderson and one of our first appointments was with pain management. Once again, the Lord provided the best as we got a teaching professional. When he heard the story of our pain management journey, he was furious and was ready to go after some people's license to practice. Lisa was moved from high dose opioids to Methadone for pain control and they started small and gradually worked up until the pain was controlled yet she was still able to think and function normally. Correcting this major issue on the first day gave us great confidence in MD Anderson and it was a good start.

CHAPTER EIGHT

Beating The Monster Is A Fight

We really loved our oncologist. He was a teaching professional (one of the best and a sought-after lecturer). He was personable, funny and caring. He gave me his personal mobile number and told me to call him any time I had questions or concerns. I respected that access and only called when something seemed off. One time I called and he was literally on a plane headed to a lecture and he apologized he could not talk but promised to call me as soon as he landed – which he did. On another occasion I called and he answered while he was lecturing. We had the best and the thought of leaving him and starting over with someone new at MD Anderson was troubling. I asked if he would stay involved and he said he would have access to her treatment plan and notes and he would monitor progress in the background. He assured me that he had arranged for us to see the best and he was confident that we were now in good hands. His reassurance was comforting though we did not want to see him go.

MD Anderson is huge. We went to the first visit early so we could learn all the basics like where to park, where are the labs, where is oncology – oh, the entire place is oncology – where is our specialty center, where is x-ray/CT/MRI and most important, where is the cafeteria and what do they serve. We found the floor where the Multiple Myeloma staff is located and learned that treatments actually take place on another floor in the facility.

Our new doctor was much younger than our other oncologist but she was very knowledgeable and had received and reviewed Lisa's entire medical history. She got right to the point. We were to start a new treatment regime involving a mix of IV and pills that had to be ordered directly from a cancer drug manufacturer. As before, labs would have to be drawn and levels approved before giving IV treatment. We would do

two IV treatments per week for three weeks while taking the pills every day. At the end of three weeks we would get a week off to let the body recover then start again. Through it all labs would be monitored to watch white cell counts since Multiple Myeloma is a bone marrow disease that affects the production of white cells. Cancer cell concentration could be monitored by watching other blood markers. The idea was to decrease the cancer markers while maintaining or improving white cell counts. When the cancer markers got low enough, we would start injections that promoted overproduction of stem cells in the body. The blood would then be filtered and the excess stem cells would be collected and counted until at least 8 million were collected. After that, a bone marrow transplant using her own stem cells would be scheduled. Initially we thought transplant would happen right after Christmas. It was late September when we started the process.

We started out this new journey with ease. My job was going well in my new department with my new boss and schedule flexibility. We managed to schedule afternoon treatment times so I could go to work early, work through lunch then leave early enough to drive home, pick her up and drive downtown. We would be travelling in the opposite direction of rush hour. Once there, labs were drawn and we waited or went for dinner until clearance was given. On nights I had praise team practice or Wednesday night church, we could get back to our side of town just in time to make practice or service. Sometimes while I was at practice, Lisa would attend evening prayer. This was an exhausting pace but I found a way to make it work and it became normal for us. When the Lord is with you, you really can do everything.

Around October 2014 things began to change. Lisa became more and more fatigued and began to complain of dizziness and chest pressure. One evening it got so bad that I took her to the MD Anderson ER. Once there they drew blood and took a chest x-ray and everything looked good except her pulse oxidation readings were 79. Normal is 94-100 and below 85 means hospitalization. One of her medications had caused a condition called methemoglobinemia. The red cells that carry oxygen within the body were being affected so they could carry oxygen but could not effectively release it to body tissue. The offending medication, one of her antibiotics (Dapsone) was discovered to be the culprit and

added to Lisa's medicine allergy list. The process to discover and reverse took a few days so she was hospitalized and treatment was interrupted. They stopped treatment since we were 2 ½ weeks into the 3 weeks on 1 week off cycle and decided to give her a few more days of rest. We visited oncology just before the start of the next cycle and everything was deemed ok and good to go.

We began the November cycle and once again, 2 ½ weeks in we were back at the ER with chest pain and breathing trouble. This time x-rays showed a blood clot in both lungs. Treatment was stopped once again, the PE (pulmonary embolism – blood clot) was treated with blood thinners and other meds. These hospitalizations were becoming an issue as she had to be healthy enough to start stem cell collection and free of infection and PEs before we could proceed with the bone marrow transplant. The transplant team was now involved and following the treatment plan with concern. By December, the transplant team met with the treatment team to discuss medical viability of a transplant. Our early Christmas gift was a decision to proceed but we could be punted from the list if additional infections or PEs appeared. The stem cell collection process was now beginning.

Injections were given of a drug that causes the body to overproduce stem cells then we came back after a few days and Lisa was hooked up to a machine that circulated her blood through a centrifuge and after the stem cells were pulled out, the blood was returned. The process was painless but because the blood was removed from the body and centrifuged at room temperature before being returned, the body temperature is lowered and you get very cold. As in teeth chattering cold even under heated blankets. The number of these collections depends on how willingly the body overproduces then gives up the stem cells. Lisa produced stem cells in record numbers and we were done with collections in just a few visits. This had to be another blessing from the Lord as were told, normally, the body produces less and less stem cells per collection but in Lisa's case she produced more at each collection so we were done in record time. They collected so many cells that she had enough for 2 transplants. The additional cells would be cryogenically banked in case we needed them in the future. Once again, the Lord knew what we would need and was providing in advance. We just did not know it.

By Christmas 2014 and New Year 2015 all was back on track and a target date for the transplant was set. Cancer levels were at remission levels, there were no PEs and no infection. It was time for me to research again – this time it was around autologous stem cell bone marrow transplants. The process was Lisa would be hospitalized in total isolation and given Melphalan which would kill her immune system completely. A few days later her stem cells would be thawed and returned to the body. The stem cells would recognize that her body no longer had bone marrow cells and they would become bone marrow cells and start to reproduce. As that happens the body once again starts to produce white blood cells and the immune system starts to rebuild. The chance of rejection is minimized by using her own stem cells but the primary danger is if any infection enters the body, there is no immune system to fight it. We had to weigh this risk and after prayer, we decided to move forward. This was going to be the answer. The Melphalan would kill all the cancer cells as well as the good cells and then she would start over with stem cells to build a new, cancer free, immune system. We were trusting God to watch over her and keep her infection free until her body was strong enough to fight on its own. The date was set and now all we had to do was stay healthy and wait.

CHAPTER NINE

Trouble In The Midst Of Trouble

New Year 2015 brought completion of a new assignment at work and I was working with my manager on next steps while keeping him informed on Lisa's condition and treatment plan. He was 100% supportive. On the HR side though, things were getting strange.

My company contracted out the administration of FMLA claims so emails and phone calls related to FMLA were coming from somewhere else in the US and not our HR department which was onsite. I began to get phone calls asking when I was going to submit hours against my FMLA case. I told them that my manager had allowed me an alternate work schedule and was supporting me on time away requests. I wanted to have an open FMLA case in case something changed and I needed to take time off beyond what my vacation and personal time off allowances could provide. For some reason, the company handling FMLA was unhappy with that response. The emails and phone calls increased in frequency and each time I explained the situation. I went to our local HR rep and was told they could not help. Eventually the phone calls and email stopped so I figured they had finally gotten the message and understood what my plan was.

Transplant date was set for February 14. With hospitalization and Melphalan on the 12th. This was going to be the most unusual Valentine's Day we had ever celebrated together. We were optimistic, scared, nervous but trusting the Lord to make it all go well. We truly believed that the Lord had guided every step through every diagnosis and every specialist to get us to this point and finally rid her body of cancer. Some healings are instant while others use doctors and the medical community. When you have a life-threatening condition, you really do not care how the Lord

causes your body to line up with the healing He gave us at the cross, you just thank Him for it.

January 29 started like any other day. I left for work after making sure Lisa had everything she needed. At the office I checked emails and contacted labs I would need access to that day to complete the latest assignment. I had been told I could move offices so I finished up the last of my packing of personal items. Out of the corner of my eye I noticed security was walking around the floor. This was never good as it indicated someone was probably going to be walked out. About then my manager walked up behind me and said I need you to come with me. Thinking we were headed to one of the labs, I grabbed my laptop and he said, no, you have to leave that at your desk. I followed him out of the office area and he headed down the hall where the HR office was – the security officer was following at a distance.

I really did not know what was going on since under FMLA my job was protected. When the HR rep told me that I had been selected for the next round of layoffs I asked her about FMLA. She said she had checked and the outside company had closed my claim saying that since I was not submitting hours against the claim then it was not needed. To "save administrative costs" they had closed the claim. Two weeks before the most important day of my married life and I get caught in a layoff.

My layoff package included 3 months of salary and benefits. After those 90 days, I could pay COBRA to keep insurance intact. At least the transplant and recovery would be covered but now I had to start a job search while going to the medical center every day. I immediately began to reach out to my professional contacts and let them know I was looking and could use any and all leads. My routine changed from juggling work and medical to handling medical by day and searching jobs boards and LinkedIn by evening. Unemployment pay was not an option because it had been less than 2 years since the last layoff. A former manager that I ran into in a grocery store parking lot reminded me that our former employer had a pension fund and if I needed to I could contact them and apply for a hardship withdrawal. I did this immediately, took the 20% hit for early withdrawal and put the money in the bank. I thought this combined with the 90 days of pay would get us through until the next job.

Meanwhile, back at the hospital, transplant day was upon us. After

Lisa received the Melphalan she was in complete isolation in a positive pressure room (filtered air flows out and nothing outside flows in) where each person entering had to completely gown up with gloves, mask and gown. While visiting, personal contact had to be kept to a minimum. On actual transplant day, a water bath thawing station was set up outside of her room and the cryogenically preserved stem cells were delivered, thawed, then placed in an IV for return to the body. The nurses and doctors told us this would be her new birthday because her system would now start over. Within 3 months she would have to start her immunizations again as if she were a new born. Her immune system was truly gone.

Though medical technology had done all they knew to do, at this point, we were in God's hands. A simple cold virus or errant bacteria could end it all. As there was no immune system for any antibiotic or medication to work with if administered. Blood tests confirmed that the white cell count was zero. Each day we would watch the blood work to monitor the white cell count to see if the transplant had taken and the body was finally producing white cells on its own. This would become our focus for the next few weeks.

On the job front, I was spending 4 hours a night reviewing job postings from every major jobs board. I do not believe in "shot gunning" where you just send to every opening and hope to get a hit. Instead, I would review every job and if I had at least 50% of the skill set then I would submit an application and record in a separate file what the job was and with who. I did this every night and even on weekends. The clock was ticking on the 90 days worth of pay and I was still paying all bills with the $1700+ per month COBRA payment looming in the near future.

At this point most people would have fallen apart. Wife in a critical medical condition, no job, denied initial public assistance and unsure what tomorrow holds. This is where the enemy start his work on your mind. Even when resting you are bombarded with all the negative things that could happen. No mental scenario you go through ends positively and if you allow yourself to stay in this mode, it leads to a downward spiral where you tell yourself it is hopeless and you are better off not being here to face it. At moments like this, having the Lord in your life and being surrounded by like-minded, positive influences is crucial. For me that was my church members and especially my friends on the praise

and worship team. When I was mentally attacked the most, I could talk with one of them and/or go to practice or service and they were there to encourage me without judgement. Daily prayer time was crucial though looking back, it was not much of a prayer time, more of a "Lord hurry up and get me out of this". It is hard to start prayer with praise and gratitude when your world is crumbling but I think the Lord understands this. Sure, He would rather us approach Him with thanksgiving and praise, but when we are hurting, I know He understands. Most important is that you continue to talk to Him as often as possible and seek guidance and peace to get through whatever you are facing. Like the saying goes, when you are going through hell – just keep going.

In week two we noticed the white cell counts start to rise, then rise rapidly. This was a sign that the transplant had taken and her body was once again building an immune system. This was great news in the midst of all the job and financial things going on. Through it all, I never lied to Lisa but I definitely sheltered her from the struggle I was facing both in the world and in the Spirit. I always assured her that we would be ok and I had this. Her job was to focus on hearing from the Lord and getting better. She did her job well and in just under 40 days her white cell count was high enough that she could be released with sterile precautions. The most difficult part of this was she desired to once again be part of the church family but we could not allow much hugging or touching. Nonetheless, we were in church just days after she was released and it was a glorious celebration as those who had stood with us and believed with us and declared her body to align with the Word of the Lord all got to see her. She was excited but also embarrassed since all of her hair was now gone and she covered her head with fashionable scarves. We were home and beginning a new chapter. We were confident that everything was going to turn in our favor.

CHAPTER TEN

Only God

The 90 days are now up and all I have in the bank is my severance package plus a cashed-out pension plan from a previous employer. I have yet to miss a bill which included, mortgage, 3 charge cards, all utilities, gas to/from the Medical Center plus parking and a hefty parent PLUS loan repayment matching my mortgage payment. The job search was going nowhere but I kept up my 4 hours a day minimum of searching in any industry segment that would allow me to stay in the Houston area. With Lisa in treatment at MD Anderson in downtown Houston, I was limiting job searches to the greater Houston area. However, I began to think maybe age discrimination was at play. I had one interview where I defined the issues they were having and offered several possible solutions only to see the offer go to someone younger and less experienced. That was one of only a few interviews I would ever get.

On the way back from a follow up appointment at the Medical Center the car began to overheat while we were in the express lane. It did not help that on that day there was an accident in the express lane that slowed and stopped traffic while I was trying to nurse an injured car back home. Once we were able to exit the express lanes, I drove directly to the dealership and dropped off the car then we took the shuttle ride home where I could get my truck. The next day the dealership called with the news, the repair would be $2500. It might as well have been $200,000 because I did not have that either in available cash or on credit. As I began to run through scenarios of what I could sell to get cash (turns out there was not much there), I took a break to go to the grocery store to get something Lisa need to make dinner. As I was checking out, I noticed they had installed a self-service lottery machine. I had never played the lottery or done scratch

cards as I did believe in it because I knew the odds were against you. But I felt an urging to buy just one ticket. It's only a dollar, what could that hurt.

The next day I was back at the grocery store; for what I do not recall. After checking out I decided to go to the machine and scan my ticket to see how we had done. The scan showed a dollar sign which meant we had won something but I could not read the amount. So, I went to the customer service counter and asked the high school aged clerk if he could scan this ticket and tell me what it was worth. He scanned the ticket then froze as if he did not know what to do. He looked at me, then the ticket then back at me. I asked, how much is it? He again stumbled and told me they could not pay out the ticket here, I would have to go to downtown Houston the lottery office to get my money. I asked, how much is it? He did not reply. So, when I got home I went to the Texas lottery website and typed in my numbers. We had hit 5 of 6 numbers on a $19 million Lotto and the payout was $2500. Just what we needed to cover the car expense. Never in my wildest dreams would I imagine that a Lotto payout would be provision.

Time seemed to accelerate and money drained from the bank account at about the same rate. The job search was hopeless. I kept track of every application I sent and at this point there were several hundred entries in my file and I had been contacted by exactly one company. I decided to be proactive with every company/organization I owed money to and I contacted them by email and/or phone and explained the situation. To my surprise, most were cooperative and offered alternatives to assist. The biggest relief, so I thought, was placing the PLUS loans on deferment through an income driven repayment plan. If your income is zero, your payment is zero until you have income again. That $1700+ per month not having to pay would allow a few more house and utility payments.

By now we had reached the summer of 2016 without missing a single payment on any debt but there simply was no money left. It was time to apply for government assistance. After all, this is the type of situation those programs were set up to handle, right? Not so fast.

Unemployment pay was denied because I had not been back to work long enough after the first and only time in my life I ever collected it. Lisa could not be declared medically disabled and collect Social Security because in her career she had worked for civil service (they do not pay into

Social Security), then self-employed and retail (which does collect Social Security), then a school district (which does not collect Social Security). Through it all she did not pay in enough quarters to qualify to file. This was especially frustrating since there are people in this country that never paid a dime into that system but they get a check every month.

So, I would start looking for part time work and apply for public assistance with medical. At this point COBRA benefits had run out and we had zero medical coverage, nothing in the bank and I had cashed out all retirement and pension accounts. We had the house, our two cars and two weeks supply of food in the freezer. To this point I had been very positive about finding employment and I had told very few people, including church and family members, of our situation. No one really knew how far we had slid and I liked it that way. You see, when I am on the job I am paid very well for solving problems no one else can. To me, this was just another challenge and I thought I would solve it. I see now that God would have to bust that pride if I were to go to the next level. I did not see it then.

Welfare assistance was denied on two separate applications. Living in a house with two cars disqualifies you because you have too many assets. I tried to explain that Lisa was still in recovery and we needed a stable, sterile environment to protect her and moving to an apartment or trailer park would not meet that requirement. We were basically told that there would be no help as long we were still in a house that we "owned" regardless of medical condition. Food assistance was also denied for the same reason. We were receiving calls from her doctors at MD Anderson telling us we had to come in for at least a blood test to see where she was in recovery. I had to decline telling them I could not even afford to pay for the gas down there or the parking fee once I got there much less the doctor fee. Harris County Texas has a medical assistance program so we decided to apply for that in hopes of getting Lisa back into treatment. As with everything else, we were denied because we had "too many resources".

One evening there was a knock at the door and I could see it was a couple on our street. We went to the door together and greeted them and asked them to please come in for a while. Through conversations I had been having with them when I would go to the mailbox or be out

doing yard work they knew everything about our medical and financial battle. We would talk often as he had also been laid off and eventually gave up and started a small business while his wife came out of child raising retirement and became a realtor. It was common to talk out on the sidewalk but them coming to the house was a little unusual. As we chatted about all things medical and job search, she interjected that they had been part of a local group for years that did community work. She talked about the various causes this group worked on and then she said the words I never thought I would hear. "We told the group about your circumstances and they voted unanimously to help you. Here is a check for $5000 and we hope it will take away some of the stress." I think at that point we all began to shed tears and a group hug was definitely in the cards. I never knew this organization existed and I never thought our neighbors really cared about what we were facing. I was wrong on that last one and another stripe was laid on the back of my pride.

I got call backs from Home Depot and Kohls about part time employment. After meeting with Kohls, it was evident they thought I was over qualified and would not be calling back. Gee, part time turn downs feel just like fulltime employment rejections.

By now we are at October and stores are setting up for Christmas sales so I was hopeful that would mean at least seasonal opportunities. So, off to Home Depot for the interview. I was told right up front in the first 10 minutes of the interview that I was grossly over qualified. I was asked why I was looking for part time work with a resume that read like mine. I explained the layoff and the medical battle and told the interviewer I was desperate to keep my utilities on and food on the table. She said she would hire me to be part of the Merchandise Execution Team if I promised to leave my brain at the door. She explained that they had ways of doing things that were dictated from corporate and if I came in trying to suggest ways to improve (she had read the black belt portion of my resume) it would make for a rough time. If I could show up every day at 5 AM and just do what needed to be done that day, I would have a job. I agreed. What else was I going to say? I needed to work for my own sanity and I need the money for food.

Leaving my brain at the door got more difficult the longer I was there. I see issues and I just have to come up with a way to make them go

away and here I was in a situation where I was basically forbidden from doing just that. Every time the frustration, the sweat, the dirt of the job would build up, I'd stop, take a breath and thank God I had some place to work. I would have to learn to praise Him through everything. With each passing day, that became harder and harder. Lisa would get up each day and play a CD of healing scriptures while she got ready and I would make time to read my Bible daily and pray. We attended every church service and I continued on the praise team and attended every practice. We were determined that no matter what, we would not turn from the Lord and daily we had to walk that out.

During work we talked amongst ourselves about the upcoming Christmas day off and what each other was planning to do. I told one associate that this would be the first Christmas in my life when there was nothing to put under the tree. I told them stories of how when we were growing up and my parents could not provide money for us kids to buy them things that we would go to my parent's bedroom or medicine cabinet and take their deodorant or combs and wrap them up so they would have something from us on Christmas morning. We were taught early that it was not the cost of the gift but the thought behind wanting to give to another.

It was the week before Christmas and the Home Depot job was full of filling stock with Christmas items that appeared to sell out as soon as they were put out. Each morning started at 5 AM with a MET meeting, followed by a warm up walk then daily work assignments. Today, however, there was a special meeting called. As I sat at the table I noticed bags of gifts and I remembered that at some point someone had asked for a contribution to the Christmas party. I felt bad at the time that I could only give a few dollars. I'm a giver who gets joy out of blessing others and this time when they came around all I could give was basically my lunch money. That came back to me as I saw the bags of gifts.

As the meeting proceeded and we had company provided refreshments my supervisor began to explain that the team had a tradition of selecting one member each year to receive the money collected for the party. I was informed that this year the team voted to select me and I was given a Visa gift card for more than $50. It was hard to hold back the tears but I managed. I was extremely grateful but at the same time embarrassed

that people making just over $10/hour would be giving me money for Christmas. I had just received another stripe in correcting my pride but the meeting was not over. One of my associates stood up to speak and he said he too grew up with little but he swore once he got on his own that he would never let anyone he knew go through Christmas with no gifts under the tree. The two bags of gifts on the table were from him and my supervisor out of their own money. They said that it might not be much but at least Lisa and I could celebrate Christmas. Provision.

As the meeting ended, I thanked everyone and asked if I could take a moment to take the gifts to the car. When I got there I just sat and cried. A flood of gratitude mixed with embarrassment and anger hit me and I could not hold it back. Thankful and grateful that those who appeared to not have much more than me financially would think of me but angered and embarrassed that I had gone from a solid six figure income to barely affording food. Another stripe on the back of my pride. But another provision orchestrated by the Lord. I took the gift card and I bought something for Lisa.

Now going into 2017 and the job search applications had crossed the 1000 application point with only 3 failed interviews. Each time I left the interview I knew I had done well and never felt like I had bombed anything. As a former hiring manager I knew the drill and all the behavioral questions. I answered everything honestly and I was sure to do my homework each time so I knew what the company did and what situations they might be facing. With no prospects in sight and now zero money, it was time to face my creditors and tell them how bad things were. I started with the charge cards and 2 of the 3 were very cooperative allowing me to suspend some payments and/or pay interest only. The third card just doubled down on reminding me what I had due and when. I reluctantly told them that if that were the case they would receive zero from me until I could regain employment.

With one card off the table, the other two under some control and the PLUS loan on income driven repayment, I set my sights on the house. I called the mortgage company and explained the situation. I told them I would be putting my house up for sale but unfortunately, they would now be getting zero payments from me until I sold it. When the agent asked

the next question, I thought he was being sarcastic and I nearly hung up on him. I asked him to please repeat what he said.

"Could you come up with $25 a month for the next 6 months to pay towards your mortgage?", he asked.

"Are you serious?"

"Yes, sir, we have a hardship program where you can pay $25 per month and remain in your home while you continue to search for employment. If you are interested, I can start the paperwork now and we can make it effective with your next scheduled payment".

"Yes, of course.", I said.

"This program is good for 6 months and if at the end of that time you are still unemployed, you can apply again but the rate will probably be different."

I accepted the offer. God had come through once again. Now about those utilities.

When God Doubled Down

The six month grace period on the mortgage was ending and when I reapplied, the $25 jumped to $350. I had to commit to accepting it to stay in the house but I knew I did not have that amount. I thought the time had come to sell the house so I posted this on NextDoor.

"Friends and neighbors, I have enjoyed being your neighbor in this community for the past 20 years, but long termed unemployment while fighting a cancer battle with my wife have left me no choice but to sell. At this point, I cannot even afford moving boxes so if any of you have some you want to give away, please contact me."

At the same time, I called my Pastor and explained the financial situation. After detailing all I had done to date we talked through selling the house. I had equity in the home but not enough to go buy a smaller place outright and if I needed to borrow the difference, I had insufficient income and a pile of debt. Renting an apartment was questionable because they really do not care how much money you have in the bank (I assumed my equity would go into the bank), what they want to see is if you are working and how much you make. Strike two. To me, there was no way out. I really felt trapped and frustrated.

Then Pastor made an offer. The church would cover my house payments and some utilities out of the benevolence fund if I could continue paying as much as I could for food and other expenses. Grateful beyond belief I accepted but inside was dying that the church where I had for so long been a tither and a giver would now be paying my bills. Stripe three on the back of my pride.

The next day I received a phone call that could only have been God arranged. It sounded like this:

"Bob, you don't know me. I got your name from the community

directory and I hope you don't mind me calling you. I feel strange saying this, I usually do not look at NextDoor but this morning during my prayer time I had a nudge to look there. I was drawn to your post and I am so sorry you are going through what you are. My husband and I want to help you."

I told her I did not mind her call but I was not sure they realized just how bad things had gotten in my finances. She explained that her and her husband had founded a charity and they wanted to help. She asked if Lisa and I would mind meeting them so they could explain. She asked if we wanted to meet somewhere public, at my house or at their home. Very reluctantly I accepted and we agree to meet them at their home the next day. Part of me did not want anyone else, especially strangers, to know just how bad things had gotten but another part of me was screaming for some relief.

The next day we drove to meet the couple that had made the offer. Since it was the same development, their house was not extravagant and absolutely nothing screamed money. They both met us at the door and invited us in. After a few pleasantries and small talk about the neighborhood they began to explain. Both had retired from Fortune 100 companies back east and had grown bored in retirement so he started trying his hand at investing and trading. At one point he thought he could get a better return on their retirement than the corporation running their plan so they withdrew some of their retirement and used it as seed in his new hobby. He proved his point by significantly beating their previous return on investment so he began to build his hobby into a business. He was so successful that they agreed to take 50% of what they made and start a charity to help others. They would only donate to charities where their funds could go directly to the needy and not to overhead. They had supported hospitals, assistance ministries, etc. but had never supported anyone directly, outside of family. They talked over the post she had read on NextDoor and agreed they wanted to help. They were offering substantial cash up front to help with immediate expenses as well as asking to pay utilities and the one charge card that had been uncooperative. We would check in with them every month and they would determine if additional help was warranted. I was skeptical and was searching my mind for the catch when she excused herself and left

while we were talking with her husband. She returned in less than a half hour and handed me several thousand dollars in cash still in the bank envelope from their bank. They would call us in 2 weeks to see how things were going. They asked how Lisa was doing and how long it had been since she had been seen.

I explained that when we applied for the highly touted Obamacare that we were accepted but the program required a monthly premium $200 more than the total amount I bring home from Home Depot and the yearly deductible was $14,400 which was more than the total I would bring home in a year working part time at $10/hour. When I inquired about subsidies, I was told we had too many assets. So much for insurance for all which I knew was a lie when it was spoken. My only benefit was I got a special number to enter on my taxes so I would not have to pay the $700 penalty for not having insurance. I had received similar treatment from Harris County and we had been turned down twice by MD Anderson for charity care. No Obamacare, no Harris Cares, we were on the nobody cares medical program. But, Jesus cares.

Each week I would write what amounted to a status report to our charity providers. I would explain what I had spent money on, how the job search was/was not going, how Lisa was doing and anything else I thought would be of interest to them. In one report I described how our stove controls had caught fire one night while I was at practice and Lisa managed to get it turned off before the kitchen ignited. I had researched the replacement control and it would be $198 if I did the labor to replace it and get the stove running again. While I was researching that, our refrigerator, (both appliances were original to the house and now nearing 20 years old), began to make really strange sounds and the freezer part seemed to be getting warmer. I was going to try to diagnose that and look at parts as well. No sooner had I sent the weekly report, I got a phone call from our charity couple. They asked what it would cost to replace the appliances. I told her if we did model for model replacement it would probably not be cheap since we had put top of the line appliances in the house when we had it built. She asked me to go price replacements and call her from the store when we had a price.

So, we went to where we had purchased the original appliances and asked what the replacement models were and a cost. I called our couple

and reported the cost was much higher than I had expected. She asked to speak with our salesman. We could see the salesman playing with his computer and relaying price information back to the person on the phone. He then stopped, said thank you and asked if they wanted to talk to me. He handed me the phone and I heard, "just do what he says and we'll talk with you soon" and she hung up. Perplexed, I asked the salesman what was up. He said, the guy on that phone just bought you a new stove and refrigerator and he added a 3 year extended warranty to each. When do you want them delivered?

Lisa and I stood there not knowing what to say. That gesture was again over $5000 AND in addition to the other assistance with expenses. Lisa and I went to the car, sat down and just broke into tears while praising the Lord. Every bad that was being thrown at us was being met with miracle and provision. Though inside I was ripped apart that I was now living and surviving on the grace of others, I knew the Lord was in it all. I so desperately wanted to return to a place where I could be the giver but I had no idea if or when that would happen.

In the next status report we thanked them again and reported that the one card I was making no payments on was making an offer but I could not accept it. They asked if I would allow them to speak to the bank on my behalf. The bank was offering to accept interest only payments and if I could make them successfully for at most 6 months then they would agree to unfreeze my card and stop reporting me as late to the credit bureaus. I simply could not afford the payment. But the charity couple called the bank and agreed to cover the payments for the next 6 months. That was over and above the utilities help and paying for replacement appliances. God had put these people in our lives for a season. Who could ever conceive that the Lord would bring in strangers to hold up your arms in a battle?

The next week we received notification from the State of Texas that our application from months back for grocery assistance had now been approved. We would be getting food assistance as long as my unemployment continued. So now, all of our financial needs had been met. Yet, I was nowhere near where I wanted to be. I wanted to work in meaningful employment where I could use my brain and be paid for doing so. I wanted to give and not receive from my church and strangers. I

began to once again tithe out of the little I made working part time at $10/hour. Part time turned into 40 hours per week with occasional overtime. I was surviving but in my eyes, not thriving.

Another neighbor, who has never come over but we have talked on many occasions, knocked at my door. He asked how things were going with the job search and if Lisa was ok. I had noticed that one of his cars was missing and that he had gotten a mini Cooper so I asked him about that. We both like cars so it was a logical conversation transition. He said he was not pleased with his Dodge Challenger so he sold it and bought the mini. His next statement still gets to me today. He handed me an envelope and said, "I sold the Challenger and here is the profit. I hope it relieves some of the stress I know you must be going through. It's not much but I hope it helps." In the envelope was $2000. And later that night another neighbor dropped off a card signed by the entire neighborhood. Inside were various gift cards to food establishments totaling $500. The Lord had provided again and just before I was hit the hardest emotionally.

On the job, I faced the most pride busting episode I could imagine. I was working in the electrical section that day at Home Depot and we had been instructed to pull all floor stock and clean the shelves and the floor under them since product was getting very dirty. Electrical was very close to receiving and the compactors so all sorts of grime was floating around and settling on product and the shelves. I was under a shelf looking like a real life version of Pig Pen from the Charlie Brown cartoons when I heard a voice say, "Bob, can you help me?" This was strange because the MET team did not usually do customer support and I knew not many people knew I was working at Home Depot. As I literally crawled out from under a shelf covered in dirt, I saw the chief technical manager from my old company. He was looking for something for a home project and had seen me there so he asked if I could help him find what he was looking for. I gladly led him to the area he needed. He never said more other than thank you. Inside I was mortified. Before being laid off I had interviewed with this gentleman to become part of his technical staff as a certified six sigma black belt researching improvements in electrical engineering concepts for new products. And now I was dirty as a pig working part time for $10/hour and he sees me in that condition. I think my pride took several stripes at that moment because that one hurt mentally for days. It still hurts to this day to recall it.

Now fall of 2017 and Lisa had not seen a doctor for over a year. She began to complain of emerging pain and just not feeling right. We would pray each day for her to feel better but she instead grew worse. One night she got so bad that she begged me to take to the ER at MD Anderson. I knew that as soon as we set foot in the ER it would be a minimum of $15,000 without insurance but she was suffering. Once again, going to the negative as is often my first reaction, I thought to myself, we saved the house thus far but this time it is gone. We got in the car and headed downtown.

The ER had all of her treatment and transplant records so her medical history was known. The ER docs questioned why we had not been back for checkups and I told them flat out that I had been unemployed for going on 3 years and we had been denied Obamacare, Harris Care and MD Anderson assistance. They proceeded with testing, said the multiple myeloma had come back and she needed to restart treatment immediately. I told them that could not happen and she was given medication to ease the pain and sent home. We reported this to our charity couple via text.

The next day our Oncologist called and said she had been notified that we were in the ER. She said we needed to start treatment immediately. I explained to her exactly what I had told the ER doctors and she asked if I had applied for charity assistance through MD Anderson. I told her I had applied and been denied twice and even gave her the name, phone number, office location and email of the person who denied us twice. She asked if I had access to a computer and she told me to apply again. Since I had already applied twice, all of our financial information was already in the system and it was a matter of reviewing it, changing the application date and hitting submit. After applying again, I could feel the pressure on me in a physical manner. I had been stressed over everything not going the way I wanted it to but I had never felt it physically. This time it just felt like no matter what I tried, something was always going to jump up and bite me. We had finally gotten finances payable and now Lisa was sick and not just sick, the multiple myeloma had come back. I went to bed but did not sleep much. My prayer time was more of a why me whining to the Lord and my mind would not shut off from trying to find a solution so I got little to no sleep. Lord you have been real in my life and I have had the pleasure of meeting you face to face so what am I missing to allow this to continue?

CHAPTER TWELVE

Better or Worse?

Within 2 days I received a call from MD Anderson. Our application for charity had been approved and any and all treatments and medical needs would now be met 100% through the end of the year. It was now September 2017. If still unemployed I could apply again in December to cover 2018. Within hours of approval, the oncologist's office called and scheduled the restart of treatment the next day at 4 PM. We were finally getting Lisa the treatment she needed and we were able to schedule afternoon appointments so I would not have to miss any time at Home Depot. My new schedule was be at work by 5 AM, get off at 1:45, 15 minutes home, shower and change, drive to downtown and be on time for 4:00 appointments. Leave downtown around 10:30 to 11:00 PM, get home and in bed by midnight to get up at 4:15 AM and do it again. We tried to schedule appointments to leave Wednesday and Thursday evenings open so we could attend midweek service and praise team practice.

It was a day off from treatment and after work I was returning from the mailbox when I saw our neighbors at my driveway. We talked about how my job search still seemed like a dead end and how working at Home Depot was just enough on top of charity and church assistance to get us through. We were surviving but not thriving. That is when they handed me an envelope. The organization they were a part of had asked them how things were going for us since they blessed us last year. When the report was that not much had changed, the organization issued a second check for $5000 and asked our neighbors to pass along that they were praying for us. God showed up again. Provision.

Several weeks into the new schedule I received a call from a company I had never done business with. They wanted to know if I was interested in interviewing back at HPE (where I had been laid off back in 2010).

They had a contract to provide personnel with specific backgrounds to targeted positions within HPE. If the interview went well, I would work directly for that company but be assigned onsite at HPE. When they told me who the interviewer was I almost dropped the phone. I was to be interviewed by a woman I had been peers with back in 1997 when I first came to Houston. The position would involve a mix of all the experience I had accumulated to date. The HPE site had flooded months before so the interview would be at a local Starbucks. By the end of the interview I had the job and they were asking how quickly I could start. I asked them how quickly they could have a badge for me and the next day I submitted my resignation to Home Depot. The mystery is that to this day I have no clue how that company found me, got my resume or knew that I would align for that job so perfectly. Provision.

The new job would have full medical benefits that would start in December since it was now October. Imagine that, a contract job with full medical benefits at a company you never applied to, doing work that you had been rewarded for doing in the past.

During the interview process I made it clear to my contract manager, my HPE manager and the team manager I would be supporting that Lisa was in cancer treatment and some days I may need to work alternate hours to work around her treatment schedule. They all seemed to understand and were very supportive. The first time I approached my HPE manager and asked about alternative hours for a certain day, she said "You have a company issued laptop and the WiFi at MD Anderson is very good. I know. My sister was there. If I were you, I would login and work remote." Not only had God provided a great job with two great companies, He also provided a way for me to work full time and care for my wife full time. God can provide in ways you cannot even dream up. I began to feel guilty over all the worry I put myself through.

Our charity couple contacted me and said there had been a huge transaction error in some of their trades and they would ask that I begin to take back responsibility for the bills they were assisting with. They had lost substantial funds and were having to cut back on their charity giving. I was more than happy to once again be responsible for my household. I had been at work for a month and a half and they were still agreeing to cover expenses so I could build up a little cushion. I was about to approach

them when they contacted me. I thanked them again the best I could and told them we were headed for another transplant. All they asked was that I keep them posted on our progress. I guess it is really is true that the Lord will bring others across our path for a season. In this case, total strangers had come along side and helped us until we could help ourselves and they were gone. Over the next few months I would send texts and emails but I did not get a response. I never heard from them again. Sometimes I am tempted to drive by their home and see if I can catch a glimpse of them. Other times I picture that they were just angels sent to minister at a specific moment and if I go by I will find they were never really there. It does not matter to me either way. I know where my help comes from and if He wants to send angels or move people to act, who am I to choose. I just need to thank Him, praise Him and know that He cares about what I go through.

Back at MD Anderson, treatments were back in full swing and immediately something was off. The usual 3 drug cocktail had been modified with a newer, more potent cancer killer and this time there were side effects that were not present before. Two weeks into treatment we had to rush back to the ER with breathing difficulty. X-rays showed blood clots in both lungs so treatments stopped, she was hospitalized and treated for PEs. After a few days she was released and we waited for the next oncologist visit before starting another round of treatments. Little did we know at the time that this cycle of getting two weeks in and being hospitalized for something would become the norm. First, PEs, then uncontrolled heart rate and blood pressure to the point where they coded her in the ER, then another condition, I asked what the end game was because we could not keep repeating this cycle. The treatment team had decided to try to get her healthy enough and drive the cancer markers down enough to do a second autologous bone marrow transplant on February 14, 2018, exactly three years to the day since her first transplant. The question was, what was making her so sick that treatments had to be stopped after two weeks.

I went back to the internet and read everything available on the new drug they had given her. After all, that was the only change from the first time when everything went so smoothly. I was convinced the new drug was the culprit but the treatment team just kept talking about how

wonderful that drug was and what a success rate it had in controlling multiple myeloma. Medical journals echoed what I was hearing from the treatment team. Finally, on the webpage from the drug manufacturer, right there in a table of probable side effects, numbers 3-5 were Lisa's medical issues. I printed out a copy of the webpage and took it back to the treatment team. I was shocked that they were unaware of this but as a result the dosage was modified and treatments were back on. God had given me the desire and the means to solve the mystery of what was making Lisa sick.

Christmas 2017 and the start of the New Year were the strangest I have ever experienced. I was optimistic that the second transplant in two months would be the answer to our prayers but the engineer in me kept going over the fact that something was not right this time. Every time I would have those thoughts, I would cast them out and remind myself that Jesus gave us healing when He took every infirmity with Him to the cross. We just had to get Lisa's body to align with the Word. If that meant using medical treatments and transplants then so be it. As hard as I tried I could never really get rid of the thought, what if this does not work this time? I wanted to treat Lisa like every day could be our last together, but the nagging thoughts of "what if" combined with the daily grind of work intertwined with medical treatments seemed to be taking me in a different direction. In my subconscious mind I was preparing for the opposite of what the Word promises and that dichotomy only added more confusion. I needed the Lord really bad at this point and rather than seek Him more, I doubled down on working through it.

My new medical benefits were now in effect so we notified MD Anderson and replaced charity care with insurance coverage. The plan carried a high deductible, the amount of which I did not have so I figured we would get started and try to make payments along the way. The first dose of the first drug given on January 3 would be $15,000. I was not sure how the drug company would cover it since I had insurance but it would not kick in until after I had met the deductible. Somehow treatments just continued uninterrupted and no one was asking for money.

January 2018 was flying by and we quickly reached a decision point. Was Lisa strong enough to undergo the stress of another transplant? Even with partial treatments, the cancer had been driven down some but

every two weeks she was being hospitalized for one condition or another. Actually, to my surprise, the transplant team agreed to accept her and the date was confirmed for February 14, 2018. Another surprise was that her latest MRI showed a tumor on the spinal column directly adjacent to where the first one was cut off the spinal cord. Radiation treatment was out of the question because the spinal cord at that location had received maximum allowable dose after removal of the first tumor. The transplant was on to not only arrest cancerous white cells but also to kill the spinal tumor.

At this point I began once again to concentrate on the finances and started asking the finance office what I owed and why I had not been billed. I was told I did not owe anything. I asked how is that possible since I never met my deductible? All I got back was, it has been paid and your insurance is paying 100% at this point. Someone or some entity had covered the $15,000 drug cost and met my deductible for the year in the process. To this day I do not know how that happened. God came through with provision once again and this time He did not let me know how or who.

CHAPTER THIRTEEN

Time To Start Anew

If the first transplant was Lisa's new birthday, it was time to celebrate that date with yet another new birthday. February 14, 2018 came around and once again we were back in MD Anderson in complete isolation watching the situation unfold as if watching a rerun. We knew what to expect because we had been here before, exactly 3 years ago. Somehow that did not make it any easier. We had now been at this battle nonstop for four years and though the routines seemed routine, the emotional and mental battles were new. The first time around, losing her hair and having to have her head shaved was more traumatic than the transplant itself. When everything began to grow back she had different hair than before and it was naturally styled. People would often ask where she had her hair done and the reply would be "God is my stylist". Well now that would have to come off again so there was emotion over that. Emotions over being in the hospital in general. Hospitals had become home for the better part of the last 4 years and this was getting old and wearing on both of us. Having no social life and no marital life due to side effects of drugs and treatments was beginning to make us seem more like roommates than a couple. I was falling more into the role of caregiver than husband and she despised that word. She forbid me from using the word caregiver around her or to anyone. We rarely fought or argued in the 36 years we were together (except for the separation period) but I noticed her picking fights over the silliest things. I later learned that was because I had checked out as a husband so the verbal jabbing was to see some kind of reaction, even if it was negative.

The 40 days in isolation passed and it was once again time to come home. We would follow up with the transplant team in a month but in the meantime, we would have a host of other follow ups since she was being treated by pain management, cardiology, hematology, GI, urology

and gynecology. We tried everything to get back to some normalcy, but meds, side effects, after effects and fatigue always seemed to get in the way. Through it all we always had the Lord. I was not understanding what we were going through but I had no doubt the Lord was there with us. I cannot imagine what it would be like to face situations like this and not have the Lord. I was all in to do whatever it took to beat this stuff, but inside it was as if I was preparing for the end.

While at MD Anderson for a cardiology follow up I spotted the transplant team head in the hallway. Since it was going to be a while before we got in to cardiology I got Lisa comfortable in her wheelchair and I walked down the hall to see the doctor. He immediately recognized me and told me he had planned to call me that day. I have learned it is usually never good news when the doctor, not his staff, wants to speak with you. It had been almost two months since the transplant and I thought this was a little early to be hearing from the doctor since we had not even been back for our post release visit. He asked if I had a few moments and if we could go somewhere to sit and talk. He was right to the point; the second transplant had failed. She was going to be sent back to oncology to restart treatments immediately.

I asked how he could know it had failed in less than 2 months. The Melphalan was supposed to kill all fast reproducing cells (cancer, hair, skin, etc.) and allow her stem cells to regenerate her immune system. Instead, the most recent PET scan revealed that the spinal tumor not only had not been killed by the Melphalan, it had grown in size and now was producing tentacles into the back side of her lung. The PET also showed new outbreaks in the bone on her hip, ribs and femur. The cancer was still there and gaining in strength. The doctor and I went back to cardiology and wheeled Lisa to a quiet place and gave her the news.

The most obvious question is, what do we do now? We asked it and were told that oncology had already been alerted and before we left the building we should stop by there and set up an appointment. Because all doctors inside MD Anderson have access to each other's treatment notes, the cardiologist already knew the results as did hematology which was the next appointment. Each doctor advised her on medications and medication changes since she would now be reentering treatment and they advised that we get back to oncology immediately. We were able

to schedule the appointment within the same week. Once there the oncologist expressed sorrow that the transplant did not work and said we would have to restart treatment. I reminded them that treatment had not gone well and that we were in the ER every 2 weeks and then admitted. And what about the tumor on the spinal column next to where her surgery had been? If it was growing into the spinal canal and the lungs it would have to be addressed and soon. The answer was to go see radiation oncology. That seems off to me since it was radiation oncology that had already determined there could be no radiation at that site. None the less, we scheduled our appointment with the doctor suggested.

The ride home that evening was quiet. I don't think either of us talked much. We just listened to Christian music and stared out the window. Both growing tired of the constant battle and neither wanting to quit, when we got home, we just held each other and cried. No words, just tears and hugs. I fixed us some dinner and afterward we talked. Lisa said she did not believe this was the end and she knew there had to be something else. I agreed to be there no matter what the path was and we went to bed. Maybe sleep could ease the pain, tension and confusion.

Radiation oncology met with us and discussed a new option. Instead of doing 3D conformal radiation they wanted to do proton radiation. MD Anderson is one of less than a dozen sites in the US that has a proton accelerator and it was used for treatments about 17 hours a day then used for research overnight. We would be scheduled for a study MRI and from that they would make molds to hold her in place during treatment and custom build proton steering molds to direct the proton radiation to specific spots while avoiding others. The penetration rate of the protons could be directed such that they could radiate the entire tumor without radiating the spinal cord that already had maximum dose radiation. The simulation and mold building would take 2-3 weeks. In the meantime, we waited, adjusted medications as needed and met with pain management since the tumor was causing pain once again. I do not know if most people will see it but through this I could see God's hand once again. The "last hope" treatment was proton radiation and we just happened to already be at one of a handful of facilities in the country that could provide the treatment. I do not believe in coincidences. I do believe in God directing our paths and leading us to be where we need to be.

The 6 weeks of proton treatments were painless but back pain continued to intensify. We were now mixing proton treatment sessions (usually late evenings, like starting 8-9 in the evening) with ER visit to address other issues. Large dark colored blisters started to appear under the breasts and on both thighs. They looked fluid filled and looked like if you poked them with a needle that water would run everywhere. They began to get sore. The pain was driving irregular blood pressure, shortness of breath and wild swings in heart rate. I seemed that we were now at the ER at least once a week and each time I would ask what the growths were and received no answer. Finally, on one visit, as the ER doctor was about to discharge us to home once again, I demanded that he look at the growths on the legs before we went anywhere. This time, this doctor seemed concerned. He asked how long they had been there and I told him weeks, but no one in any department cared to look at them. He canceled the discharge orders and decided to do a needle biopsy of the growths. After a few hours of waiting for lab results he told us that she would be admitted. The growths were not fluid filled as expected but were more solid and he wanted to notify oncology. She would be admitted and treated by IV for pain.

The next day was when everything changed. I was at work when I received a call from Lisa.

"These people are trying to kill me," she said.

"What people?", I asked

"These nurses and the people who work here". I could hear as she had put the phone away from her mouth and was yelling, "You! The blonde! Get in here now! I know what you are doing! You won't get away with this!"

"Who are you yelling at?"

"They thought they could get away with this but I know what they are doing".

I told her, "I'm leaving work right now and I will come straighten this out. Hang up the phone, turn your back to the door and do not say anything to anyone until I get there. Do you understand?"

"Yes."

"Promise me you will do what I said and I'll be there in 30 minutes."

We hung up and I immediately ran out of the building at work and

headed downtown. Lisa was mild mannered and would rather pray for a stranger than yell at them. I had rarely heard her raise her voice to anyone the entire time I had known her. Something was very wrong if she was screaming at people and especially at people who she should have known were there to help her. I pressed the speed limit on the way into the city not knowing what I would face when I got there. As I was driving, the phone rang. Caller ID said it was Lisa so when I answered I just said, "I told you I was on the way."

"Mr. Pemberton?", asked the voice on the other end of the phone.

"Yes, this is Bob, who are you?" I asked.

"This is Lisa's doctor. Mr. Pemberton, are you aware of what is happening here?"

"I know something is not right and I am on my way there. I'm about 15 minutes out right now."

"So, you have spoken with her this morning?"

"Yes. She was not making sense."

"Did you happen to tell her anything?"

"Yes, I told her to put her back to the door and not talk to anyone until I get there."

"Well that explains a lot."

"What's wrong?"

"She knows that I am her doctor but she will not talk to me. She told me to wait until her husband got here so I asked if I could call and talk to you by phone."

"Can you hand her the phone?"

"Yes." And there was a pause before I heard Lisa's voice say "Hello."

Playing along with her conspiracy theory I said, "This doctor is one of the good ones and she will help us get all those others. Go ahead and tell her what is happening and I will join you shortly. I'm nearing the parking garage."

I hurriedly parked the car and all but jogged the nearly quarter mile of hallways to her room. As I arrived, the doctor was just coming out. She suggested that we go in together. She told Lisa that her behavior was concerning and that they wanted to be see if there was a medical cause for it. They would do a spinal tap to be sure she had not picked up an infection that would affect her brain. To my surprise, they had already

ordered the kit and the procedure would happen right there in the room. As we waited for the kit to arrive at the room, the doctor motioned for me to step outside.

Outside the room she told me that the lab results were back on the growths and they were myeloma that had spread to soft tissue. Her concern was that it may be in her spinal fluid or growing on her brain. A spinal tap would reveal if the spinal fluid was carrying anything. She asked if I knew what a spinal tap was. I told her yes, because I had gone through the procedure when I was younger. She then asked if I had a reaction to needles. I said no. She asked if I would mind staying in the room and keeping Lisa calm while she did the tap. I agreed.

So, with Lisa sitting on the edge of the bed facing me and the doctor behind her, we set pillows on the bed table so Lisa could extend her arms and lean forward while I held her hands and tried to keep her still. I was looking directly at Lisa but just beyond her ear was the doctor prepping the area with sterile covering and sterile solution.

"First we are going to numb the area so you may feel a little stick followed by a temporary sting.", she said.

"OK, now you might feel some pressure but whatever you do, try not to move."

"Great, got it on the first try…. and here comes the first sample.", she said as she lifted the first vial up to the light for both of us to see. She then placed the vial in a holder.

"Number two has started and this is flowing great. At this rate we will be done in record time. Remember to keep as still as you can."

"And number two is done", she said as she lifted the second vial and was staring at it in the natural light coming through the window. I saw it the same time she did and she knew that I knew what I was looking at so she motioned to me to not comment with a finger to the lips and a shake of her head.

Spinal fluid is one of the most pure liquids on earth. Completely colorless and particle free. If you draw fluid and you can see impurities with the naked eye, you have contamination and that is not good. Vial two had something floating in it.

"Number 3 started and flowing nicely. You are such a good patient and this is not taking any time at all."

Vial three was presented and this time she put a gauze behind it. I could see both discoloration and particles. The doctor looked directly at me and shook her head. This was not looking good at all.

"Number 4 started and you are doing fantastic. I know you have been in that position a while now but try not to move and we will be done shortly."

The final vial was as cloudy as the third.

"OK, we are done but still don't move. I want to be sure the needle is out and everything is fine."

After clean up and helping Lisa to lie down in bed, I met the doctor outside of the room.

"Doc, I know that fluid was supposed to be clear, so, what does this mean?"

"I cannot comment until I know for sure, but we are going to send these vials to cytology and let them analyze what is in them. It's the weekend so we probably will not get results until Monday."

"I know you cannot say anything on the record but what is your gut feel on what you see?"

"With the unusual behavior we saw this morning, by the way she seems fine now, I suspected something affecting the brain. There is obviously something going on in the spinal fluid and if I had to guess I would say the cancer has spread to her spinal fluid or to the brain."

"So, what would that mean?", I asked.

"Let's be sure we know what we are dealing with before we start to speculate."

"What else could be in the fluid?", I asked.

"The labs will tell us for sure and we will talk then." The doctor excused herself and told me they would be in touch. They had my mobile number if they needed to reach me.

I went back into the room congratulated Lisa for being such a good patient. She looked at me and began to cry.

"What's happening to me? I heard people talking saying I had done some not nice things and I'm not like that. I couldn't have done what they were saying. I would remember that if I did."

I told her, "With all the medicines and treatments, your body chemistry is wacked. I'm not surprised you could do something strange

and not remember it. That's why you are here – where they understand these things and can help you. They know this may not be the real you they occasionally see, but they understand and will help you anyway."

"I'm so sorry if I hurt anyone. I don't want to hurt anyone. I have to tell them I'm sorry."

"Everything is fine. You stay in bed and rest and I will talk to them. I will explain it to them. Everything is fine."

I got her calmed down, made sure she had ordered dinner and when it arrived I left to drive home. Now I was scared and for the first time in this entire battle I actually entertained the thought of what will I do if she does not make it. It was like once I let the thought in, I could not shut it off. My mind raced through notifying the kids, funeral arrangements, service preparation, notifying creditors, calling friends and family The entire way home was a blur of thoughts I did not want to have but could not stop. Now I was getting mad at myself for planning for the loss of my wife of 36 years when she was very much alive and resting at the hospital. I was exhausted when I reached home but I went to bed so I could get up in the morning and go just spend time with her. I feel like my faith took a hit because suddenly believing that the Lord would touch her and we would truly see miraculous healing was replaced with not knowing what tomorrow would bring.

I visited her all day that Saturday and between church services on Sunday. I texted my manager and told her I would go directly to MD Anderson on Monday morning instead of reporting to the office. We were expecting very important lab results and I wanted to be there when the results came in. She agreed and asked that I keep her informed of the results. This was not a formal request, we were friends who had known each other for over 20 years and she was truly concerned.

At the hospital room waiting for doctors to make rounds, I was very quiet. Lisa asked me what was wrong and I just said, the job has got me distracted. That was not a lie but it was not the real reason I was quiet. I just did not want to think about what was next or how to explain it to her until I knew something for sure.

When the doctor arrived, she was not alone. This was not unusual since this was a teaching hospital but these folks did not look like interns. She asked Lisa if she was ok and how she was feeling today. She asked if

she felt that she was able to think and understand as things were explained to her. Lisa said yes and the doctor began

"The lab tests on the growths showed that the myeloma has spread to soft tissue. You know that the last PET scan showed new growths on the ribs, pelvis and spine. We did the spinal tap on Friday and sent the fluid for cytological analysis and the results show that the cells in the spinal fluid are cancerous."

At this point I interrupted and asked, "So what is the treatment for that?"

"There is no treatment for that. The medical center here in Houston is the largest medical complex on earth and you will not find anyone here who is even researching treating cancer in the spinal fluid."

There was silence as Lisa and I just stared at each other.

"So what happens now?", Lisa asked.

"There are very few treatment options left. We are recommending transfer to hospice. We can treat the tumors with radiation only to try to keep them from growing and to address pain but know that we will do that for pain relief only and not working towards a cure."

I added, "This is the Houston Medical Center. We are at MD Anderson, the leading cancer research hospital in the country and you are telling me have no more options? So, what kinda time frame are we looking at here if she goes to hospice? Are you sure there is nothing else?"

"No one can ever say for sure, but based on what we have seen we estimate 2-4 weeks in hospice. There is one final thing we can try but the treatment is brutal and there is a good possibility she might not survive the treatment."

"With treatment, how much time?", I asked.

"At most 2-4 months." She replied

Lisa spoke up and said "No! No more treatments. No more treatments."

My brain was trying to process what just happened. On the outside I heard things like signing DNR, termination of treatment and reviewing hospice providers but on the inside I kept telling the Lord, no, this is not what Your Word says will happen and this will not be the end. Our miraculous healing will just have to happen at home where the medical community cannot take credit for it. I just kept telling the Lord, no, this is not where it ends. You brought us too far to end it now. This is not the end.

In the meantime, others had showed up at the room and were bring us information on hospice, what that meant and a list of providers. We had to sign legal forms and when I stepped in to sign since I had medical power of attorney, I was told no. Lisa was alert and fully understood the situation, she would have to sign them herself. But she did not want to. When it came to DNI/DNR I had to explain that this was not a surrender but more like an insurance policy. No one ever expects to use insurance but you have it in case you ever need it. This would only come into play if needed and at that point there would be no need to prolong anything. She reluctantly signed then looked at me and said, "Why do I feel like I just gave up?"

I assured her she had not given up. I told her, "As long as the Lord is on our side, this fight is not over. Instead of relying on medicine we need to rely 100% on the Lord now."

I called my daughter who is a BSN and told her the news. Her and her husband would leave from their home immediately and drive the 2.5 hours down to meet me at my house. The next day we all went to the hospital to see Lisa and to interview different companies who were candidates to provide hospice care. Lisa was happy to see her only daughter and trusted the advice she would give as a medical professional. So, we listened to presentations from three hospice providers. I immediately focused on one but did not say anything. When they were all finished and had left, we discussed as a family which seemed to be the best. After some back and forth discussion, the family arrived unanimously at the same one I had focused on. It was time to relax and wait for discharge the next day. It was July 4, 2018 but I really did not feel much like celebrating or even watching fireworks which could be seen from the hospital windows. A mix of exhaustion, anger but a strange peace hit me. I just wanted to go home and sleep.

CHAPTER FOURTEEN

Provision To The End

July 5th, we came home and were to meet our chosen hospice company at the house that afternoon. Lisa had many questions about what her routine would be and Rebecca had a slew of medical questions and "what ifs". I was just praying that all would go well. The Lord had provided at every step of this journey and I expected him to be with us until He could take her home.

Provision comes in unexpected forms as we have already seen - having access to the absolute best doctors, strangers stepping in to help with finances, getting jobs you never applied to, having access to treatments only available at a few places in the country. But how could there be provision in the last days of someone's life? Remember that work remote permission? Now I could work from home and be there full time for the last days. Even though we were now in hospice care, I was not about to miss a single minute.

When the chosen hospice company representatives showed up for the first time they were amazing. Caring, compassionate, yet thorough, they went over every aspect of the program including a timeline of what to expect and how to deal with it when it happened. They arranged for all necessary medical equipment and medications to be delivered right to our door and explained when and how to use everything. In addition, they offered to send in professionals to assist with personal hygiene and attend so I could leave the house to run errands or go to the office just for a change of scenery. That may not sound like much, but at this stage of the process that is a huge mental relief.

Rebecca took a leave from her job to be home with her mother. This was a double blessing since she was also a BSN registered nurse. Her help was invaluable as the physical body began to deteriorate and we had to assist Lisa with everything including even getting in and out of bed. As

pain increased so did the medications and we soon reached a point where we did not know if Lisa was really communicating with us. One moment she would be clear as if nothing was wrong then the next time you were unsure if she knew where she was. Rebecca was used to this from her work in the hospital, but this was mom and that made it different. I could see the tension building. I guess others could too.

On one visit, the hospice nurse took Rebecca aside and asked her how she was doing. That was unseen provision. They talked professional to professional and even cried woman to woman. Rebecca got a ton of questions answered and had reassurance that her mom would not be in pain and would receive the absolute best care until she left us. That tension relief at a time when you do not even realize how tight you are is truly a blessing from above.

About a week in, we started to notice changes. I called Lisa's sister and told her if she wanted to visit, now would be the time as opposed to later. She made arrangements at her home and boarded a plane to come visit. A nudge from the Holy Spirit told me to call her. The timing of the visit was perfect since Lisa was still very communicative and alert at that point. By the end of the visit her sister could see a noticeable decline. They had a great time talking and reminiscing and you could see it was good for both of them. At one point in the visit, while Lisa was sleeping, her sister and I sat and talked. We talked for hours and were in amazement that in the 37 years we had known each other that we had never once just sat and talked. She thanked me for everything I had done for her sister and said the entire family shared her feelings.

I was confused by that but it was not the first time I had heard something like that. To me I was just doing what I made a vow to the Lord to do. I did say for better for worse, in sickness and in health, so, how could I do anything different? Well, evidently, I was the exception. I was told by MD Anderson personnel how amazed they were that I was there for every appointment, every treatment, every test, visiting every day when she was hospitalized. They told me that the norm was marriages either ended with the start of cancer treatment or the patient was systematically abandoned and was left on their own. I was told on numerous occasions that I was a good husband. Each time I heard that, I could not conceive of doing anything different. How could someone just abandon the one

they love when things were not going as planned? I know I have never been one to automatically go along with the "guys", but I never dreamed that dedication to your wife, family or church was optional in the eyes of others. In retrospect, I guess in a way I was provision for Lisa. I hope she knew that I was doing it because I wanted to and not because I had to.

After her sister left, Lisa and I had a talk while alone. She asked me point blank if she was going to die. I tried to side step the issue and told her that was between her and the Lord. What came next still bothers me to this day. You see, I'm a fixer. When things go wrong I fix them. I am rewarded nicely on my job for being able to find and fix things that most would not. I carry that attitude into my home life and even my church volunteering. It suddenly hit me that this time I was not going to fix this. I remember looking Lisa in the eyes and telling her, "Hun, I've tried. God knows how much I've tried. But, I can't fix this. This is well beyond me and what happens next is between you and the Lord. You have to talk to Him and see what's next because I just don't know. I'm so sorry." I began to cry on her chest. "I love you and I always have but I can't fix it this time. I can't fix it." I began to weep as we held each other. She tried to assure me that she knew I had done everything I knew to do. She said I love you then told me if she died she would expect me to go on and find someone else. She did not want me to be alone.

At this point our church family stepped in and took it to a whole new level. They set up a schedule of volunteers to come and sit with Lisa in 4 hour shifts so I could at least have the break of going to the office. They cared for her, fed her, prayed with her and while she was resting they read scriptures to her. They gathered around her and acted like the four crazy friends in the Bible who broke a hole in the roof where Jesus was talking to lower down their sick friend. They spoke healing over her and commanded her body to line up with the Word of the Lord. No one asked them to do this. They volunteered then set the schedules and coordinated the rest.

When it was unclear how much longer Lisa could communicate, we called our son and asked him to please come home. He flew in that night as his employer was very understanding. As soon as he arrived, Lisa perked up and though only able to communicate sparsely, she wanted him to sit and talk with her and she wanted her hugs. The whole family was

now together and as we talked amongst ourselves, all agreed that this was the most difficult thing we had ever faced. Our faith said the Lord could heal her with a word, but all of us having science related degrees could also see what was playing out in front of us and faith quite often battled with reality. We spent as much time as possible with her and with each other. We took care of her and cooperated in any way we were asked when hospice personnel came to the house. We worked in shifts somewhat so if someone needed to just get out of the house they could and another would cover. We were a team. We were a family.

My son told us he had reached the end of his allotted time away and he would have to leave. This was hard for him since none of us knew when the time would come. He wanted to be here but had to get back. He kissed his mom, told her he loved her and I drove him to the airport. Somehow, I just knew that was the last time he would ever speak to his mom but we did not talk about that. I returned home and went to bed. All was well and Lisa was resting. All meds were up to date, she was in a comfortable position and it was time to rest.

The next morning when I awoke, I was hesitant to check on her because somehow I knew she would not be alive. When I walked past her bed and could hear what sounded a little like snoring, I was relieved and headed to the kitchen to dose out her morning medications. While there, I thought I heard her wake so I went to say good morning. She was not waking but gasping. I quickly checked the "stages of death" chart hospice had provided and we had reached that point. I ran upstairs and woke Rebecca, simply stating, it has started. She knew what I meant and came down immediately. Like the instructions said I called hospice and the nurse on duty asked questions then told me to go to the refrigerator and prepare the dose of the medicine as we had been instructed. Since it was unclear if Lisa could swallow I had to deliver the medicine in a syringe between the cheek and gum so it could get into her system. It is never easy watching someone die and especially someone who was the mother to your children and your lifelong partner of 36 years. Rebecca, James and me gathered chairs around the bed and took turns holding her hands and talking to her. Trying to be positive and as calming as possible, we finally began to talk about what Lisa's day was going to be like. Oh! What a glorious day when she gets to see Jesus face to face. We were

talking about all the family and friends she would get to join up with and how happy they would be to see her. At that point, there was a gasp, then nothing. Rebecca began to cry and said I won't believe it until I hear it and she got her stethoscope and listened for a heartbeat. About the time she said she thought she heard something we could hear a deep breath and Lisa's head turned to look at us. With eyes open, that was it. The journey here on earth had ended and the glorious rest of eternity with our Lord and Savior had begun. 8:15 AM, July 18, 2018.

We called hospice and they told us to cover her so we would not have to look at her and a nurse would be there as soon as possible. Official time of death would have to be recorded by the hospice nurse after examination. It took 1 ½ hours for someone to get across town to us. That seemed like the longest wait in history. In the meantime, I called my son, my pastors and her sister. Since Lisa's mom was in questionable medical condition I did not want to call her but wanted family there to break the news. While waiting we contacted the crematorium that we had chosen in advance and they were on alert but would have to officially hear from hospice about certification of death.

The hospice nurse arrived, conducted the examination and made the declaration. Rebecca assisted the hospice nurse in cleaning and preparing the body. She was told by the nurse that doing so was unnecessary, but Rebecca insisted in helping mom one last time. The team from the crematorium arrived within an hour of hospice and after Lisa's body was removed, we began to gather medical equipment that had been provided and then met with the hospice nurse who witnessed the destruction of all narcotics and controlled substances that had been necessary. Strange how efficient the aftermath is, within 24 hours there was no sign of anything hospice related in the house.

As Rebecca, James, Phillip and I began to clean up the house and sort through things we were shocked. In the strangest places we would find cash. In drawers, taped under drawers, in shoes, in underwear, you name it, we found cash. We had no idea Lisa had stashed cash or why. As the amount of cash began to grow we began to wonder just how long this stashing had been going on and why. Did she put cash away then forget she had or was she planning for something? As the cash neared $1000, I got a little bit mad that there were cash stashes in the house and we had just

gone through a period where we needed church help, charity and food stamps to survive. How long had this been going on? We continued to find cash until the total reached $1700 – the amount needed for cremation and an urn. The Lord, through Lisa has provided for her final expenses.

CHAPTER FIFTEEN

Provision Of A Different Kind

So, what do you do on your first day alone in over 36 years? If you're me you work. I thought getting right back into things would minimize the hurt. After a day or two I went back to work where they were shocked to see me and told me I should go home. I told them I could not sit at home and do nothing, it would drive me crazy. I would do my job, make up for the days I had already taken off and in between I would plan a funeral. Since cremation was involved there was no rush to have a service so I had time to plan. Since almost all the extended family resided in Virginia, I would try to have a service here in Houston for immediate family, coworkers and church family, then fly back east and have another service there. The best laid plans often do not happen.

The service in Houston went off without a hitch. Provision continued to roll in as we were able to get the church, volunteers provided refreshments and all the immediate family got paid time off from their employers to attend. The service was led by my senior pastor who rarely does funerals anymore. This struggle and Lisa's faith had touched him as well as everyone who stood with us in our church. This one was personal. I had prepared a slide show to music of Lisa's life and it was shown as part of the service. Because she loved our church and our praise team so much, the service included a live song from the praise team with pastor leading. I was told I was excused from playing that day but I insisted. Playing with my praise team had gotten me through the battles of the past 5 years so I wanted the start of my new journey to begin with them as well. The service was wonderful and her friends, coworkers and neighbors who were not part of our church could feel the love our church had for her and the love she had for our church.

There was one brief story from the service that defined who Lisa was. We were at MD Anderson and Lisa was fairly sedated on a gurney in the

hallway outside a diagnostic test. She was resting when they wheeled in a gentleman and parked him in the same hallway across from us but fairly close. As he laid back on his gurney he let out a mild groan as in pain. Lisa woke up, sat up and says to the man, "I need to pray for you". She took his hand and prayed one of the most Holy Ghost inspired prayers of healing you could imagine. He said thank you and she laid back down and was out again.

Plans to go back east did not go well. It was frustrating to me and my daughter that every time we picked a date, someone would come up an excuse why they could not do it that weekend. After four or so iterations, we picked a date and told family that was the date and if they did not show up it was on them. They had plenty of time to reschedule events. So the date was set and I prepared all the legal documents that would allow me to transport remains by plane. When the weekend finally arrived, a major hurricane shut down most airports on the east coast south of Maryland. We could not fly in no matter how much we wanted to. To this date, neither my daughter, my son nor I know why the Lord did not want us to have a service back east. We attempted to reschedule several more times and nothing ever seemed to work out. The Lord had a reason we were not to go there and I am confident He protected us from something. I just don't know from what.

As months went on we were approaching the first holiday season with someone very important missing. I still had my contract job and was slowing climbing out of the debt hole that 3 years of unemployment while fighting cancer can dig for you. The kids had returned to their homes and jobs and we were beginning to talk about how/where we would gather for the holidays. At work, the program I was supporting finally shipped so I knew it was time to start looking for something else, but what? I notified my contract house that we should start inquiring about what was next and then I waited. While waiting I got a call from someone I had worked with in another division of HPE. He suggested an opening that he was currently temporarily filling and said I was perfect for the role. I would report to a manager I had been peers with some 22 years earlier and that was not a problem because I knew him and liked him. The problem was the next level manager and I had a history and I could not stand the

thought of having to work for him again. None the less, I was convinced to at least apply for the role then see how the interviews went.

I notified my contract house and my HPE manager that I was going to interview. HPE told me they were working on a conversion req to transfer me from contract to a permanent employee. I asked what the req number was so I could apply and all I heard was we are working on it. So, I began the interviews with the new division while waiting to hear about the conversion req. During the interviews I was told that I seemed like a good fit for the role and I was asked if I had any reservations about the new job. I relayed that I had a history with a certain person who was prominent in the organization and I relayed my horror story of how we parted company. People could not believe that things were that bad between us but reminded me, that was over 20 years ago and people and circumstances change. They suggested I set up a meeting with this manager and just talk through opportunities in his organization. If there was still history present then I would have to decide if I could work through it or withdraw from the job application. If, however, things went well then I would have a clean slate to start a new role. I took them up on that advice and scheduled the call. I will not go into details of what was said, but I can say the Lord showed up and set us both at ease.

I finally heard about the conversion req and I was not happy. They were offering less than my contract rate and I was fed up with taking salary cuts just to get jobs. I was hesitant as to whether I should even apply. As with any major decision I went to the Lord in prayer. I prayed that it would become clear which direction I should take. Two days later I was contacted by the recruiter for the other division job. Though they could not meet my request for restoring time in grade and subsequent vacation time, the offer was 15% higher than my contract rate and I would be positioned to move to the next grade as soon as an opening occurred. I would be hired the week of Thanksgiving which would mean I would get the long weekend to be with my family and be paid for it as well. Provision was continuing.

As things began to find some sort of normalcy and I was in a position to not work constantly, my mind began to wander and I guess the grieving process was finally knocking at my door. I told myself if I just stayed busy then everything would be ok. Grieving was for those who did not

know the Lord and were unsure where their loved one was. Well, I was wrong. Grieving is necessary and it happens to everyone, no matter your belief system. I began to miss Lisa and the fact that she was not here after everything we had been through was making me mad. I was lonely, exhausted and tired all at the same time. My prayer life became more questioning than praise and petition. I would often say, "Lord, Your Word does not lie, but her healing never came." Or I would say, "Lord, Your Word does not lie, but more than two agreed and you still did not grant our petition." Or, "Lord, Your Word does not lie, but it looks like Your name was not above the name of cancer. Lord help me to see what I am missing."

This continued for about a month and each time I did not get an answer, I got a little more upset. I reached a point where going to praise team practice, which I live for, became an obligation and hearing anyone, including my own pastors, preach on the healing power of the Lord made me want to run out of the church. We had done everything and done it by the book. I mean the Holy book. We laid on hands and declared healing in Jesus name. We anointed with oil. We prayed together. We pleaded our case using scripture as evidence that cancer had to leave. Lisa started every day listening to healing scripture read as she recited along with the CD. We never missed a single service or practice unless it was absolutely necessary and in every service we asked for corporate prayer for healing. We continued our giving either through time and talent or financially when it was possible. We volunteered for church events and continued serving various church ministries. We did everything possible to keep the Lord front and center in spite of the worldly circumstance. I could feel my faith being tested and I had nothing to fight back with. I finally reached the point where I asked the Lord to just take me home. If I was too stupid to hear from Him and to do what He wanted me to do, then I'd be better off out of here and someone else could finish the task He assigned to me. I did not like these thoughts. I did not like these feelings.

In prayer before bed one night I was doing my usual "Lord Your Word does not lie" when I had the distinct feeling someone was in the room with me. I looked up and it was Lisa! She was in a white gown and much younger. I had never seen her look more beautiful. She smiled at me and whispered, "It's ok. It's ok." As she put her hand out to me, I was ready

to take it and join her if I could. Before I could touch her or hold her I realized she was not alone. A voice came from behind me and said, "She is with Me now and everything is ok. You do not have to worry." I started to speak and ask why, when I heard the word perspective. I asked, "what do you mean, perspective?" No answer and they were gone.

I had comfort in seeing Lisa healed, happy and beautiful but why was the answer to my questions – perspective? I could not get that out of mind. On one hand I was wondering why the Lord would appear to me with Lisa to comfort me. Who was I to deserve that? Billions seek that opportunity and do not get it. On the other hand, what did perspective mean. Several times a day I would pray and meditate on – perspective. Finally, after two weeks, I prayed, "Lord, please forgive my ignorance but I just do not know what you have said to me. What does perspective have to do with my questions on why Your Word did not seem to work?" Then I heard His voice again, as if He were in the room with me.

"Why do you call me a liar?', He asked in a stern voice.

"Oh no, Lord, I would never call You a liar!", I said out loud.

"In your own words you said, 'Lord, Your Word does not lie, but', since My Word does not lie, there can be no but. My Word does not lie, you just need to change your perspective."

"Lord, I do not understand."

"Did you pray that she would be free of cancer and that the damage it had done to her body would be eliminated? Did you pray that her body would be made whole again?"

"Yes, Lord, I did."

"You saw her and she has a completely new body. There is no cancer and no deficiencies. Did you pray that she would grow closer to Me and hear from Me?"

"Yes, Lord, I did."

"She is with Me forever now. I answered every one of your prayers and you did not see it. My Word did not lie, I answered and you were looking from the wrong perspective."

"Lord, teach me to see through Your eyes."

He was gone. I was left feeling like kid who had just been sent to his room and feeling horrible that the Lord would think I would call Him a liar. I had a lot of repenting to do and some serious prayer and

meditation on the Word to try to see it from a new perspective. What else had I missed by looking at it wrong. My brain went into overload mode and I just went to sleep. Looking back, the Lord taking time to talk to me, correct my thinking and show me Lisa was ok was provision for my mental and spiritual well-being. I still have a way to go because to this day, hearing preaching on how the Lord heals still bothers me. I guess that means I am still a work in progress.

After the visit from the Lord and many sessions where I would cry almost uncontrollably, anywhere, at any time, I thought the grieving process was over. I thought I had managed to literally work through it and it was time to move on. Then while talking to Rebecca, she asked if I would consider seeing a counselor. I thought this was a strange question and I told her no, I had the Lord so I did not need to talk to anyone else. She asked me to think about it. The next day my son called and asked how I was doing. I told him fine and we talked about hobbies we had in common and each other's job. At the end, before he hung up, he asked if I thought I needed to see a counselor. This was completely out of line with anything I expected him to say. I gave him the same answer I gave Rebecca and he said, it's not going to hurt you to talk with someone. I asked why and he said, "because we watched the cancer take you down with her." I asked, what do you mean and he said go talk to someone who can answer that. And we hung up. So, the next day Rebecca called on another subject and I asked her why she thought I needed to see someone, her answer was shocking, "because we watched the cancer take you down with her." I asked, what do you mean and she said go talk to someone who can answer that. I told her that was exactly what her brother said, and she said then maybe you ought to listen to him. Not what I wanted to hear but I really began to wonder what they were seeing… or not seeing in me.

Using the Employee Assistance Program at work I was able to schedule an appointment with a Christian counselor and was able to get in that week. So, I went to the counselor and explained everything that had happened over the past 5 years and of course, she wanted me to go back to the beginning from when I first met Lisa. It was hard reliving the whole experience and reminiscing about both the good times and the bad but if it would answer the question, I was willing to do it. She was so in-depth that it took at least two sessions just to go over all the

background and history. Tears came out of nowhere when talking about what I thought were routine subjects. That was not like me so maybe there was something I had been missing.

What came out of the early sessions was that I had become so engrossed in Lisa's treatment that I had lost myself. Every conversation with the kids was an update on treatment or research or the issue du jour. Except for church, I had no social life. I never took time for or even considered what I wanted and as a result, I stopped smiling, joking, showing interest in anything that my kids had to say. I had become mentally and socially numb. My kids wanted their dad back. No one knew the person I had become and I never saw the change.

It was time to move on, but how? What does that even mean? My counselor asked me point blank, "Who is Bob? What does he want? What does he like to do?" I was stunned that the first answer that came to mind was, I am Lisa's husband. The counselor said, "There is a problem. She has gone to Heaven and you are here. So, now, who are you and what do you want?" My first response was I did not know. Then after thinking a bit, I said, "I just love being married and having someone to share things with. I really have never been one to go out with the guys. I married my best friend and I just enjoyed spending time together." Maybe this was the first clue to how to move forward. Once again, God had provided wisdom through my kids to alert me that I needed help and then He provided a Christian counselor who could cross the bridge between psychology and spirituality. His provision had not ended with the passing of Lisa and my reemployment. So what was next?

CHAPTER SIXTEEN

Provision Is Blessing

I figured if I enjoyed being married then I guess I better start looking for members of the opposite sex to build a relationship. I have always believed in finding a friend first then dating second. But where to start when you're 62 and had been married to the same person for 36 years? Widows and singles at church? That seemed awkward. Online sites? I had heard the horror stories but figured why not give it a try to see if those stories were true. Well, they were. Out of reading profiles of literally hundreds and picking a few (about 5) to actually meet, I soon found out this was not going to be the way to find someone. Of the five, three were a nice date out with another person but absolutely no spark. One strung me along and lied to me and one was a just psycho. People, I mean stalking making stuff up psycho. Off of the dating sites it was.

A friend gave me Terry's phone number. I was told she was an independent, Christian woman who was crazy about her kids and grandkids. That did not sound like a bad combination so I bit and called her. Our first conversation lasted hours until her phone battery began to die and we had to hang up. I had no clue what she looked like or even where she lived but I could hear a smile in her voice and there was something different about her. There was a spark just talking to her. So, we talked a few more times, each time learning more about our shared love of music, church and family. Those are definitely not bad things to have in common.

One Saturday morning I was at Home Depot. My next door neighbor who had been such a help during the down times had been diagnosed with stage 4 pancreatic cancer. The fence and the gates between our homes had gotten pretty bad so I was going to replace them so he had one less thing to worry about as he struggled in his treatment. I was in the store buying supplies when Terry called and asked what I was doing

that day. I told her and she said that her and her son had just put up a fence at their house and she would come help me if I wanted the help. I told her if she was serious then I would text her my address but it would be a strange first meet because I would be in work clothes and a bandanna. She told me not to worry because she too was not going to dress up but would come ready to work. So, the first time we ever saw each other was when she pulled up in front of my house to work. I had already started and was fairly dirty and already sweaty. That did not seem to matter and we both got right to work tearing down the old fence and digging out old fence posts. Before I knew it 8 ½ hours had gone by and we had worked the entire time except when she left to get us some lunch. We talked, joked, laughed and on occasion I would pray in tongues over particularly stubborn fence posts. She found that amusing. I was so into trying to finish that I never realized how hard she was working right beside me. Add hard worker to the growing list of things I knew about her.

I soon learned that Terry was a hard worker in other areas as well. She had owned two gym franchises and had survived some unpleasant circumstance which resulted in a divorce. She was an accomplished piano player and vocalist who had both toured with her musical parents and had written several worship songs for her church. She was fun and crazy in a good way. When I met her grandkids, the older ones warned me that she was crazy. When they would introduce her to their friends, they would say, "This is my grandma, we call her Onny and she is crazy." But crazy fun was exactly what I needed and the Lord knew that. If I was going to get my personality back, I would need someone who made me feel playful – silly – joking – crazy – and able to show love again.

We agreed to visit each other's church to support one another and to see if we were getting the same messages. That was a positive as my church friends took to her and her church friends seemed to like me. One service this gentleman gets up from his seat before service and comes over to me and says, "I'm so glad someone finally put a smile on her face." Then he just walked off and sat down. I looked at Terry and asked her how bad was she before she met me. We both had a laugh and to this day do not know what he was talking about.

One Wednesday when she had visited my church for evening service I walked her out to her car and was saying goodbye. It seemed like everyone

in the church who came out wanted to come over and talk to us. When the last person finally left and it was just us and security who was closing the gates, I decided to try a test kiss by just brushing the lips while saying goodnight. I had no idea how she would react and I was scared to death to do anything to offend her. Having respect for the one you want to be with is an important trait for healthy, Godly relationships.

She was always so positive and happy that I began to call her Sunshine. She loved my eyes so she nicknamed me blue eyes. Sometimes I would meet her friends at church and they would call me blue eyes because she had never given them my name. Everything was falling into place, even music. I was listening to a new releases playlist on Spotify when I came across a song that I swear I could have written myself. The lyrics described us to a tee so much that I looked up the artist and wrote them a note thanking them for the song. "The Way You Smile", a duet by Newsong with Francesca Battistelli.

On Memorial Day weekend I went with Rebecca and James to Garner and Los Maples state parks to get a change of scenery and do some hiking. I felt like a teenager because every night I would call or text Terry to send her pictures of my adventures during the day. I could not wait to hear her voice so on the nights when text service was all I could get, I was sad. On the drive home we talked for several hours and agreed to meet as soon as I got back in town. That was the first real kiss, not some attempted peck on the lips in a church parking lot.

Our first date, the fence, was April 27 and by July I knew the Lord had once again provided what I needed. Still I was hesitant and I did not know why so I called to talk to my younger sister. It was at her house in Virginia that I had met Lisa in July 37 years earlier. I told her how Terry and I met, the fence story, and everything I had learned about Terry. So, she asked me what was wrong. To her it sounded like I had met the perfect person. After thinking a bit, I told her, Terry is different in every way from anyone I have ever known. She talks different, thinks different and looks different. I had some warped picture in my mind of what the next person in my life would be like and she was not that, even though I was immensely drawn to her and knew from the start that I loved her. My little sister turned prophetic and she said, "Maybe God is giving you exactly what you need and not what you think you want. He has not let

you down to this point and I don't think He is going to let you go astray now. If what God wants for you is not what you think you need, then you need to get with God and find out why." I was shocked by her answer but somehow, I knew she was right.

Two days later I had a meeting with the counselor and I told her how I was feeling about Terry and about the conversation I had with my sister. To my surprise, she was fairly brutal. She said, "How dare you as a Christian man judge someone by their outward appearance! That is not in the Word! That is shallow, that is pride and you need to get it under the blood immediately! You need to repent and ask forgiveness." Well, I paid for someone with a solid Christian background and I paid for someone who would cut me no slack – that is exactly what I got. She went on to tell me that from what she had heard, Terry was brave to have met me the first time in work clothes. It showed she either had confidence that seeing her at her worst could only get better from there or she was testing me to see if I really cared about her and not external things. She told me not to feel pressure to move on but to thank the Lord for who he had brought into my life. I felt horrible. I began to wonder how many other beautiful people I had shunned in my lifetime just because they had not met my artificial standard. I prayed and I repented. I asked the Lord to help me see through a different set of eyes. This was yet another stripe on the back of my pride.

The next time I saw Terry I knew without a doubt she was my gift from God. I wanted to propose but had zero funds to get a ring. We had stopped at a jewelry store one day while shopping and I was asking questions about what styles she liked. To my surprise, she said I prefer simple and elegant. She did not want the stone that takes a year's salary to pay for, she wanted simple but not plain. The next week I went to my Jared and started scouting. I found a set that I thought Terry would like and I already had the diamond so that would save a bit. I got a price which was great since the set was on closeout but it might as well have been a million dollars. I just did not have it.

A few weeks went by and as I was driving down one of the main roads here, I heard a voice that said, "Go to Jared". I shook it off since I had no money. I drove a little further and I heard it again. So, I started renouncing the devil for putting false thoughts in my head. The third time I heard it,

the voice said "Go to Jared, today!" Ok, so maybe there is something I'm supposed to be doing here, I thought. I was only two miles away so I drove to Jared and asked about the set I had spotted before. They had my profile online so they looked up the set and told me it had been sold since it had been on clearance. I was about to walk out when the salesperson said, "Wait, I believe we have some very similar and they too are on clearance." I turned around and went back to the counter to see a set that was better than the first one I had picked out. It was also reasonably priced and then the kicker, this was the last day of the 20% everything in the store. You see, there was a reason the voice told me to go today. I explained my credit situation and was completely honest about what I had been through and why. They ran a credit check and approved me for 4 times the amount I needed. I gave them her ring size, drove home to retrieve the diamond, took it back and asked if the rings could be ready by Saturday. They said they would so I arranged to pick them up by 5 PM that Saturday, July 27.

God had provided once again. I was not even looking to be able to buy a ring and was hoping I could get one by her birthday in October. At this point I knew I wanted to be with Terry, sooner than later, but I thought money was an issue. Now that the ring was possible, I had to decide how to get it to her in a way that she would appreciate. We had joked that I was her knight in shining armor so I had contemplated renting a suit of armor and walking into her church after service and doing the whole down on one knee thing. I had looked into this and I could find no costume or stage production shops in the entire area who had full suits of armor for rent. So, on to plan B. She loved church and she loved music so maybe I could pull something off during her church service and better yet during the song service. Well, there was church the evening of July 27. Since our first date was on April 27 I wanted to continue the 27 theme whenever I could. Tonight was going to be the night but I had no clue how.

I dressed for church and headed to Jared to get the finished products. They were more beautiful than I thought when I picked them out and more importantly, they met her requirement of simple but elegant. I placed the box containing both the engagement and wedding bands in my left suit pocket and headed to meet her at church. I knew where she would be because we always sat in the same seats. I arrived just as service was starting and they were opening with songs so as I held her left hand in

my right hand, I fumbled in my left pocket with the other hand to blindly open the box and feel for which one was the engagement ring. The song was perfect! The lyrics were about Christ's love for His church and how we should hold onto the things we love. As I went to pull the ring out, I accidently dropped it into my pocket. Quick, I thought, find the ring. But instead my fingers seemed to turn to jelly and I could not tell what I had in my fingers. Frustrated, I sat down and Terry did too. I finally regained control of the engagement ring but now the song had ended. I thought I had blown it for sure. When the next song began and the lyrics were about Christ claiming His bride, I knew the time was now. The Lord had provided the perfect opening for me and I had muffed it so now I had a second chance. While we were singing along, I quietly took the ring and placed it on her ring finger without saying a word.

Terry quit singing, looked at the ring, looked at me, looked at the ring and said, "Is this what I think it is?" I said, "Well what do you think it is?" Her friend who always sits beside her had noticed something was going on so she had slipped her phone out of her purse was taking pictures. Terry turns to her friend and just raises her hand and starts to cry. When she looked back at me I could not tell if she was speaking in tongues or was actually trying to say something and it was not coming out. She was crying, laughing, trying to talk and maybe even trying to sing all at the same time. As the songs ended, Terry sat next to me and started taking pictures of her ring and texting them to her adult kids and other family members. Her daughter replied back, "So did he actually ask you?"

Terry looked at me and said, "Did you ask me to marry you?"

Jokingly I said, "Do I really have to? Why else would I put the ring on your finger?"

"Yes, you do.", she replied.

"Well, in that case, will you marry me?"

And the laughing, crying, talking mix started over again. By this time people in the church knew something was going on by the slight commotion so I whispered to Terry that maybe we should just sit and listen to the rest of service. She held my hand tightly regularly raising both our hands so she could get a better look at the ring. I reached over and whispered, "I never heard your answer" as I gave her a hug and smiled. By the end of service people were coming up to congratulate us.

Turns out that Terry's friend texted pictures of the ring to ladies in church who had then texted others. The secret was out and God had once again provided – the setting, the song, the second chance, the friends and family to give blessings, well wishes and congratulations.

People I never knew existed came out of the woodwork wanting to help plan the wedding. My family back in Virginia wanted to meet Terry and started planning a huge extended family gathering at my younger sister's house. Time was now accelerating. We were so sure the Lord had brought us together that we set out to find a wedding date. Carrying on the 27th theme we looked for when the 27th fell on a Saturday. That would not happen until June of 2020 and neither wanted to wait that long so we picked October 26 but set the wedding start time for 12:27 PM. We would preserve the special meaning of 27 one way or another.

Terry and I each took time off from work and flew to Virginia for the family gathering. While there I even asked permission to stop by and visit my former mother-in-law and asked if she wanted to meet Terry. They said yes and we were joined by Lisa's sister and her husband during the visit. The visit was great and everyone liked Terry. One of her favorite past times is cooking so she shared recipe ideas with them and learned some inside cooking tips on cooking Italian. They gave us their blessings and well wishes and we told them they would be invited to the wedding. I knew they would not come because in their medical condition it was very difficult to travel. Nonetheless, the invitation would be given and I knew there were no hard feelings from Lisa's side of the family about me moving on with life.

We went back to the family gathering and it was huge. Nephews and their families, friends, old acquaintances, my sisters, their friends and lots and lots of blue crab and shrimp with all kinds of homemade sides. As often will happen with provision from the Lord, there comes the counter attack from the enemy. This time it was Terry's health. As we tried to meet and greet she got more and more withdrawn which is definitely not her personality. She had been in a car wreck nearly 20 years ago and they had placed plates in her spine to stabilize it after she broke her neck in the accident. Something was going wrong there and she had debilitating headaches and was losing use of her arm. She tried to fight it off and took breaks to go inside and lay down but it grew worse. I tried to convince her

to go to the ER but she kept saying her insurance was not good outside of Houston. Finally, I went to my sister and asked what was the closest ER. She went inside to talk to Terry and convinced her to go to the ER as soon as we got the last guests to leave.

My sister drove us to the ER she thought was best of the three close by and to my surprise, when we got there, there was almost zero wait. We were checked in in under 20 minutes and in a room in less than 30. Within 40 minutes of arriving we had been seen by the triage nurse and Terry was in x-ray. The young doctor who came in was personable and had an excellent bedside manner. She explained that the x-ray showed bone growth along the plates and she suggested that as soon as we returned to Houston we contact her surgeon and have the area looked at in more detail. She was able to prescribe medication for pain and some muscle relaxers to relieve the tension in the area. We were discharged with prescriptions in less than two hours. Most would say we were just lucky but I know inside it was yet another form of provision. Provision does not always have to be money. Provision can quite often be favor and this time it was favor.

We stayed another day then flew back to Houston to our jobs and to serious wedding planning. We were now less than 45 days out from the big day and Terry was insisting on doing the cooking for the reception. There were nearly 300 people invited and she insisted on doing all the food with her, her daughter and her sisters.

The days flew by and once again we saw provision. We were able to get the satellite church from Terry's main church on the date we needed it, with use of both the sanctuary and the banquet facilities and at a great price. Terry's dress was found on close out saving us lots of cash. I wanted to do something special so I bought lumber and built a backdrop for the alter that looked like an arched fence. It was finished on time with the help from my future brother-in-law who came and sweated it out in my garage with me as we assembled it.

Terry and I had discussed doing "The Way You Smile" during our service as a duet since it had become as much a part of our relationship as the fence and the number 27. We each rehearsed our part then agreed that there would be enough going on that day. Terry asked some of her musician friends at church and they agreed to learn and perform our song

during the ceremony. To my surprise, they also performed a song that Terry had written years earlier. Music was a big part of the beginning of our lives together.

My friend and associate pastor had a free schedule that weekend so he was able to travel to the wedding site and do the ceremony for us. Terry's sisters were able to join us the week before and share in the cooking which took the coordination of a relief effort to pull off. All family members including my younger sister who NEVER flies anywhere were able to get time off from work and fly in to join us. Every aspect of this wedding just fell into place and it came off without a single hitch and in only 3 months to the day since the proposal. Some would classify that as a miracle, I see it as continued provision.

The Lord had been with me every step of the journey but sometimes I was so engrossed in the details that I never saw it. Even before Lisa's death, others had encouraged me to write these things down because they thought others needed to hear them. I have learned the hard way that when the Word says in Hebrews 13:5 NKJV "For He Himself has said, 'I will never leave you nor forsake you'", He means it. My perspective may have been off from time to time but His Word remained true. Provision from the Lord for those who believe, comes in many forms. We just have to believe in our hearts that His Word is true and be open enough to receive when He provides. I have also learned that provision and pride do not coexist. When seeking Divine provision, pride has to go. Trust in the Lord with all your heart and with all of your soul and He will provide. In Matthew 6:25-34 NIV the Lord speaks to us and says

[25] "Therefore I tell you, do not worry about your life, what you will eat or drink; or about your body, what you will wear. Is not life more than food, and the body more than clothes? [26] Look at the birds of the air; they do not sow or reap or store away in barns, and yet your heavenly Father feeds them. Are you not much more valuable than they? [27] Can any one of you by worrying add a single hour to your life[a]?

[28] "And why do you worry about clothes? See how the flowers of the field grow. They do not labor or spin. [29] Yet I tell you that not even Solomon in all his splendor was dressed like one of these. [30] If that is how God clothes the grass of the field, which is here today and tomorrow is thrown into the fire, will he not much more clothe you—you of little

faith? [31] So do not worry, saying, 'What shall we eat?' or 'What shall we drink?' or 'What shall we wear?' [32] For the pagans run after all these things, and your heavenly Father knows that you need them. [33] But seek first his kingdom and his righteousness, and all these things will be given to you as well. [34] Therefore do not worry about tomorrow, for tomorrow will worry about itself. Each day has enough trouble of its own.

My answers were right there in His Word all along. I just needed a different perspective and to accept His provision.

ABOUT THE AUTHOR

Robert Pemberton is an Electrical Engineering graduate of Virginia Tech who built a career in quality, test, diagnostics and management in the power, defense and computer hardware development industries. He has taught as an adjunct professor of computer science at the college level and has lectured and tutored Science and Math at the high school and middle school levels. Robert was married for 36 years before losing his wife to cancer. He is now remarried and has a combined family of five adult children and four grandchildren.

Robert is an active member of the Glorious Way Church where he has been mixing sound and making system improvements for over twenty years. He returned to his musical roots by teaching himself to play bass guitar and joining the praise team, turning control of the soundboard over to people he trained using a book he authored for volunteer church sound operators titled "Sound Systems for Houses of Worship – Getting Started". Robert also authored "The Light of Heaven", a true account of his experience in Heaven after dying during a treatment for a disease.

When not supporting his church through praise team and directing all thigs audio, Robert is a Senior Program Manager at Hewlett Packard Enterprise. Outside of work and church, Robert enjoys helping Terry decorate their home and going to events to support the grandchildren.

Printed in the United States
By Bookmasters